Presented to:

Myself

By: _____

Date: _____

The Living Bible

The Bible Promise Book

A Barbour Book

Leatherette Edition ISBN 1-55748-598-4

Published by   Barbour and Company, Inc.
              P.O. Box 719
              Uhrichsville, Ohio 44683

EVANGELICAL CHRISTIAN PUBLISHERS ASSOCIATION MEMBER

The Living Bible, copyright 1971 ©
Used by permission of
Tyndale House Publishers, Inc., Wheaton, IL 60189.
All rights reserved.

Printed in the United States of America

Contents

Anger

Jehovah is kind and merciful, slow to get angry, full of love.

Psalms 145:8

But you are a God of forgiveness, always ready to pardon, gracious and merciful, slow to become angry, and full of love and mercy.

Nehemiah 9:17

His anger lasts a moment; his favor lasts for life! Weeping may go on all night, but in the morning there is joy.

Psalms 30:5

Dear brothers, don't ever forget that it is best to listen much, speak little, and not become angry; for anger doesn't make us good, as God demands that we must be.

James 1:19, 20

Don't be quick-tempered — that is being a fool.

Ecclesiastes 7:9

A short-tempered man is a fool. He hates the man who is patient.

Proverbs 14:17

It is better to be slow-tempered than famous; it is better to have self-control than to control an army.

Proverbs 16:32

A quick-tempered man starts fights; a cool-tempered man tries to stop them.

Proverbs 15:18

A hot-tempered man starts fights and gets into all kinds of trouble.

Proverbs 29:22

Stop your anger! Turn off your wrath. Don't fret and worry — it only leads to harm.

Psalms 37:8

Keep away from angry, short-tempered men, lest you learn to be like them and endanger your soul.

Proverbs 22:24, 25

A soft answer turns away wrath, but harsh words cause quarrels.

Proverbs 15:1

Fathers, don't scold your children so much that they become discouraged and quit trying.

Colossians 3:21

If you are angry, don't sin by nursing your grudge. Don't let the sun go down with you still angry — get over it quickly.

Ephesians 4:26

A wise man restrains his anger and overlooks insults. This is to his credit.

Proverbs 19:11

Better to live in the desert than with a quarrelsome, complaining woman.

Proverbs 21:19

But I have added to that rule, and tell you that if you are only angry, even in your own home, you are in danger of judgment!

Matthew 5:22

Stop being mean, bad-tempered and angry. Quarreling, harsh words, and dislike of others should have no place in your lives. Instead, be kind to each other, tender-hearted, forgiving one another, just as God has forgiven you because you belong to Christ.

Ephesians 4:31, 32

Dear friends, never avenge yourselves. Leave that to God, for he has said that he will repay those who deserve it. [Don't take the law into your own hands.] Instead, feed your enemy if he is hungry. If he is thirsty give him something to drink and you will be "heaping coals of fire on his head." In other words, he will feel ashamed of himself for what he has done to you. Don't let evil get the upper hand but conquer evil by doing good.

Romans 12:19–21

If your enemy is hungry, give him food! If he is thirsty, give him something to drink! This will make him feel ashamed of himself, and God will reward you.

Proverbs 25:21, 22

But now is the time to cast off and throw away all these rotten garments of anger, hatred, cursing, and dirty language.

Colossians 3:8

Belief

"For God loved the world so much that he gave his only Son so that anyone who believes in him shall not perish but have eternal life."

John 3:16

"And all the prophets have written about him, saying that everyone who believes in him will have their sins forgiven through his name."

Acts 10:43

God warned them of this in the Scriptures when he said, "I have put a Rock in the path of the Jews, and many will stumble over him (Jesus). Those who believe in him will never be disappointed."

Romans 9:33

But to all who received him, he gave the right to become children of God. All they needed to do was to trust him to save them.

John 1:12

"There is no eternal doom awaiting those who trust him to save them. But those who don't trust him have already been tried and condemned for not believing in the only Son of God."

John 3:18

"And all who trust him — God's Son — to save them have eternal life; those who don't believe and obey him shall never see heaven, but the wrath of God remains upon them.''

John 3:36

They replied, ''Believe on the Lord Jesus and you will be saved, and your entire household.''

Acts 16:31

''I have come as a Light to shine in this dark world, so that all who put their trust in me will no longer wander in the darkness.''

John 12:46

Jesus replied, ''I am the Bread of Life. No one coming to me will ever be hungry again. Those believing in me will never thirst.''

John 6:35

''If I can?'' Jesus asked. ''Anything is possible if you have faith.''

Mark 9:23

Then Jesus told him, ''You believe because you have seen me. But blessed are those who haven't seen me and believe anyway.''

John 20:29

''How earnestly I tell you this — anyone who believes in me already has eternal life.''

John 6:47

Charity

God blesses those who are kind to the poor. He helps them out of their troubles. He protects them and keeps them alive; he publicly honors them and destroys the power of their enemies.

Psalms 41:1, 2

When you help the poor you are lending to the Lord — and he pays wonderful interest on your loan!

Proverbs 19:17

"Instead, invite the poor, the crippled, the lame, and the blind. Then at the resurrection of the godly, God will reward you for inviting those who can't repay you."

Luke 14:13, 14

"Sell what you have and give to those in need. This will fatten your purses in heaven! And the purses of heaven have no rips or holes in them. Your treasures there will never disappear; no thief can steal them; no moth can destroy them."

Luke 12:33

To despise the poor is to sin. Blessed are those who pity them.

Proverbs 14:21

Give generously, for your gifts will return to you later.

Ecclesiastes 11:1

He gives generously to those in need. His deeds will never be forgotten. He shall have influence and honor.

Psalms 112:9

Happy is the generous man, the one who feeds the poor.

Proverbs 22:9

"For if you give, you will get! Your gift will return to you in full and overflowing measure, pressed down, shaken together to make room for more, and running over. Whatever measure you use to give — large or small — will be used to measure what is given back to you."

Luke 6:38

If you give to the poor, your needs will be supplied! But a curse upon those who close their eyes to poverty.

Proverbs 28:27

Every one must make up his own mind as to how much he should give. Don't force anyone to give more than he really wants to, for cheerful givers are the ones God prizes.

2 Corinthians 9:7

It is possible to give away and become richer! It is also possible to hold on too tightly

13

and lose everything. Yes, the liberal man shall be rich! By watering others, he waters himself.

Proverbs 11:24, 25

I have been young and now I am old. And in all my years I have never seen the Lord forsake a man who loves him; nor have I seen the children of the godly go hungry. Instead, the godly are able to be generous with their gifts and loans to others, and their children are a blessing.

Psalms 37:25, 26

Feed the hungry! Help those in trouble! Then your light will shine out from the darkness, and the darkness around you shall be as bright as day.

Isaiah 58:10

Tell those who are rich not to be proud and not to trust in their money, which will soon be gone, but their pride and trust should be in the living God who always richly gives us all we need for our enjoyment. Tell them to use their money to do good. They should be rich in good works and should give happily to those in need, always being ready to share with others whatever God has given them.

1 Timothy 6:17, 18

I want you to share your food with the hungry and bring right into your own homes those who are helpless, poor and destitute. Clothe those who are cold and don't hide from relatives who need your help. If you do these things, God will shed his own glorious light upon you. He will heal you; your godliness will lead you forward, and goodness will be a shield before you, and the glory of the Lord will protect you from behind.

Isaiah 58:7, 8

Give it to the Levites who have no inheritance among you, or to foreigners, or to widows and orphans within your city, so that they can eat and be satisfied; and then Jehovah your God will bless you and your work.

Deuteronomy 14:29

Jesus felt genuine love for this man as he looked at him. "You lack only one thing," he told him; "go and sell all you have and give the money to the poor — and you shall have treasure in heaven — and come, follow me."

Mark 10:21

"Take care! Don't do your good deeds publicly, to be admired, for then you will lose the reward from your Father in heaven. When you give a gift to a beggar, don't shout about it as the hypocrites do — blowing trumpets in the synagogues and streets to call attention to their acts of charity! I tell you in all earnestness, they have received all the reward they will ever get. But when you do a kindness to someone, do it secretly — don't tell your left hand what your

15

right hand is doing. And your Father who knows all secrets will reward you."

Matthew 6:1–4

"Then I, the King, shall say to those at my right, 'Come, blessed of my Father, into the Kingdom prepared for you from the founding of the world. For I was hungry and you fed me; I was thirsty and you gave me water; I was a stranger and you invited me into your homes; naked and you clothed me; sick and in prison, and you visited me.' Then these righteous ones will reply, 'Sir, when did we ever see you hungry and feed you? Or thirsty and give you anything to drink? Or a stranger, and help you? Or naked, and clothe you? When did we ever see you sick or in prison, and visit you?' And I, the King, will tell them, 'When you did it to these my brothers you were doing it to me!' "

Matthew 25:34–40

There are three things that remain — faith, hope, and love — and the greatest of these is love.

1 Corinthians 13:13

Children

They replied, "Believe on the Lord Jesus and you will be saved, and your entire household."

Acts 16:31

"For Christ promised him to each one of you who has been called by the Lord our God, and to your children and even to those in distant lands!"

Acts 2:39

And all your citizens shall be taught by me, and their prosperity shall be great.

Isaiah 54:13

For I will give you abundant water for your thirst and for your parched fields. And I will pour out my Spirit and my blessings on your children.

Isaiah 44:3

But when Jesus saw what was happening he was very much displeased with his disciples and said to them, "Let the children come to me, for the Kingdom of God belongs to such as they. Don't send them away! I tell you as seriously as I know how that anyone who refuses to come to God as a little child will never be allowed into his Kingdom." Then he took the children into his arms and placed his hands on their heads and he blessed them.

Mark 10:14–16

Children are a gift from God; they are his reward. Children born to a young man are like
sharp arrows to defend him. Happy is the man
who has his quiver full of them. That man shall
have the help he needs when arguing with his
enemies.

Psalms 127:3–5

Your wife shall be contented in your home.
And look at all those children! There they sit
around the dinner table as vigorous and
healthy as young olive trees.

Psalms 128:3

But he rescues the poor who are godly and
gives them many children and much prosperity.

Psalms 107:41

They have many happy children.

Job 21:11

An old man's grandchildren are his crowning glory. A child's glory is his father.

Proverbs 17:6

Children's Duties

Children, obey your parents; this is the right thing to do because God has placed them in authority over you. Honor your father and mother. This is the first of God's Ten Commandments that ends with a promise. And this is the promise: that if you honor your father and mother, yours will be a long life, full of blessing.

Ephesians 6:1–3

You children must always obey your fathers and mothers, for that pleases the Lord.

Colossians 3:20

"But as to your question, you know what the ten commandments say — don't commit adultery, don't murder, don't steal, don't lie, honor your parents, and so on."

Luke 18:20

" 'Cursed is anyone who despises his father or mother.' And all the people shall reply, 'Amen.' "

Deuteronomy 27:16

The Lord also told Moses to tell the people of Israel, "You must be holy because I, the Lord your God, am holy. You must respect your mothers and fathers, and obey my Sabbath law, for I am the Lord your God."

Leviticus 19:1, 2

" 'Honor your father and mother (remember, this is a commandment of the Lord your God); if you do so, you shall have a long, prosperous life in the land he is giving you.' "

Deuteronomy 5:16

Young man, obey your father and your mother.

Proverbs 6:20

A wise youth accepts his father's rebuke; a young mocker doesn't.

Proverbs 13:1

Only a fool despises his father's advice; a wise son considers each suggestion.

Proverbs 15:5

The character of even a child can be known by the way he acts — whether what he does is pure and right.

Proverbs 20:11

Happy is the man with a level-headed son; sad the mother of a rebel.

Proverbs 10:1

If young toughs tell you, "Come and join us" — turn your back on them!

Proverbs 1:10

Young men who are wise obey the law; a son who is a member of a lawless gang is a shame to his father.

Proverbs 28:7

"And so, young men, listen to me, for how happy are all who follow my instructions. Listen to my counsel — oh, don't refuse it — and be wise."

Proverbs 8:32, 33

My son, how I will rejoice if you become a man of common sense. Yes, my heart will thrill to your thoughtful, wise words.

Proverbs 23:15, 16

Listen to your father's advice and don't despise an old mother's experience.

Proverbs 23:22

The father of a godly man has cause for joy — what pleasure a wise son is! So give your parents joy!

Proverbs 23:24, 25

Comfort

God is our refuge and strength, a tested help in times of trouble. And so we need not fear even if the world blows up, and the mountains crumble into the sea. Let the oceans roar and foam; let the mountains tremble!

Psalms 46:1-3

Though I am surrounded by troubles, you will bring me safely through them. You will clench your fist against my angry enemies! Your power will save me.

Psalms 138:7

The Lord is my fort where I can enter and be safe; no one can follow me in and slay me. He is a rugged mountain where I hide; he is my Savior, a rock where none can reach me, and a tower of safety. He is my shield. He is like the strong horn of a mighty fighting bull.

Psalms 18:2

"For he has not despised my cries of deep despair; he has not turned and walked away. When I cried to him, he heard and came."

Psalms 22:24

If they fall it isn't fatal, for the Lord holds them with his hand.

Psalms 37:24

The Lord is good. When trouble comes, he is the place to go! And he knows everyone who trusts in him!

Nahum 1:7

The godly shall be firmly planted in the land, and live there forever.

Psalms 37:39

Give your burdens to the Lord. He will carry them. He will not permit the godly to slip or fall.

Psalms 55:22

"I have told you all this so that you will have peace of heart and mind. Here on earth you will have many trials and sorrows; but cheer up, for I have overcome the world."

John 16:33

"Come to me and I will give you rest — all of you who work so hard beneath a heavy yoke."

Matthew 11:28

You can be sure that the more we undergo sufferings for Christ, the more he will shower us with his comfort and encouragement.

2 Corinthians 1:5

All who are oppressed may come to him. He is a refuge for them in their times of trouble.

Psalms 9:9

For the Lord will not abandon him forever. Although God gives him grief, yet he will show compassion too, according to the greatness of his loving-kindness. For he does not enjoy afflicting men and causing sorrow.

Lamentations 3:31–33

Don't be impatient. Wait for the Lord, and he will come and save you! Be brave, stout-hearted and courageous. Yes, wait and he will help you.

Psalms 27:14

Contentment

A cheerful heart does good like medicine, but a broken spirit makes one sick.

Proverbs 17:22

Stay away from the love of money; be satisfied with what you have. For God has said, "I will never, never fail you nor forsake you."

Hebrews 13:5

When a man is gloomy, everything seems to go wrong; when he is cheerful, everything seems right!

Proverbs 15:15

A relaxed attitude lengthens a man's life; jealousy rots it away.

Proverbs 14:30

Do you want to be truly rich? You already are if you are happy and good.

1 Timothy 6:6

Don't envy evil men but continue to reverence the Lord all the time, for surely you have a wonderful future ahead of you. There is hope for you yet!

Proverbs 23:17, 18

God's Correction

Young man, do not resent it when God chastens and corrects you, for his punishment is proof of his love. Just as a father punishes a son he delights in to make him better, so the Lord corrects you.

Proverbs 3:12

"How enviable the man whom God corrects! Oh, do not despise the chastening of the Lord when you sin. For though he wounds, he binds and heals again."

Job 5:17, 18

He helps us by punishing us. This makes us follow his paths, and gives us respite from our enemies while God traps them and destroys them.

Psalms 94:12, 13

Yet, when we are judged and punished by the Lord, it is so that we will not be condemned with the rest of the world.

1 Corinthians 11:32

That is why we never give up. Though our bodies are dying, our inner strength in the Lord is growing every day. These troubles and sufferings of ours are, after all, quite small and won't last very long. Yet this short time of distress will result in God's richest blessing upon us forever and ever!

2 Corinthians 4:16, 17

"For when he punishes you, it proves that he loves you. When he whips you it proves you are really his child." Let God train you, for he is doing what any loving father does for his children. Whoever heard of a son who was never corrected?

Hebrews 12:6, 7

Our earthly fathers trained us for a few brief years, doing the best for us that they knew how, but God's correction is always right and for our best good, that we may share his holiness. Being punished isn't enjoyable while it is happening — it hurts! But afterwards we can see the result, a quiet growth in grace and character.

Hebrews 12:10, 11

Courage

Don't be impatient. Wait for the Lord, and he will come and save you! Be brave, stout-hearted and courageous. Yes, wait and he will help you.

Psalms 27:14

For the Lord loves justice and fairness; he will never abandon his people. They will be kept safe forever; but all who love wickedness shall perish.

Psalms 37:28

But now the Lord who created you, O Israel, says, Don't be afraid, for I have ransomed you; I have called you by name; you are mine.

Isaiah 43:1

"Don't be afraid!" Elisha told him. "For our army is bigger than theirs!"

2 Kings 6:16

Trust in the Lord instead. Be kind and good to others; then you will live safely here in the land and prosper, feeding in safety.

Psalms 37:3

He gives power to the tired and worn out, and strength to the weak.

Isaiah 40:29

So cheer up! Take courage if you are depending on the Lord.

Psalms 31:24

I know how to live on almost nothing or with everything. I have learned the secret of contentment in every situation, whether it be a full stomach or hunger, plenty or want; for I can do everything God asks me to with the help of Christ who gives me the strength and power.

Philippians 4:12, 13

Death

Even when walking through the dark valley of death I will not be afraid, for you are close beside me, guarding, guiding all the way.

Psalms 23:4

O death, where then your victory? Where then your sting?

1 Corinthians 15:55

The godly have a refuge when they die, but the wicked are crushed by their sins.

Proverbs 14:32

And since by his blood he did all this for us as sinners, how much more will he do for us now that he has declared us not guilty? Now he will save us from all of God's wrath to come.

Romans 5:9

Since we, God's children, are human beings — made of flesh and blood — he became flesh and blood too by being born in human form; for only as a human being could he die and in dying break the power of the devil who had the power of death. Only in that way could he deliver those who through fear of death have been living all their lives as slaves to constant dread.

Hebrews 2:14, 15

"With all the earnestness I have I tell you this — no one who obeys me shall ever die!"

John 8:51

For this great God is our God forever and ever. He will be our guide until we die.

Psalms 48:14

My health fails; my spirits droop, yet God remains! He is the strength of my heart; he is mine forever!

Psalms 73:26

But as for me, God will redeem my soul from the power of death, for he will receive me.

Psalms 49:15

He will swallow up death forever. The Lord God will wipe away all tears and take away forever all insults and mockery against his land and people. The Lord has spoken — he will surely do it!

Isaiah 25:8

Shall I ransom him from hell? Shall I redeem him from Death? O Death, bring forth your terrors for his tasting! O Grave, demonstrate your plagues! For I will not relent!

Hosea 13:14

But the good man — what a different story! For the good man — the blameless, the upright, the man of peace — he has a wonderful future ahead of him. For him there is a happy ending.

Psalms 37:37

That is why we never give up. Though our bodies are dying, our inner strength in the Lord is growing every day.

2 Corinthians 4:16

"So that anyone who believes in me will have eternal life."

John 3:15

For I am convinced that nothing can ever separate us from his love. Death can't, and life can't. The angels won't, and all the powers of hell itself cannot keep God's love away. Our fears for today, our worries about tomorrow, or where we are — high above the sky, or in the deepest ocean — nothing will ever be able to separate us from the Love of God demonstrated by our Lord Jesus Christ when he died for us.

Romans 8:38, 39

Enemies

Because they trust in him, he helps them and delivers them from the plots of evil men.

Psalms 37:40

"Those who hate you shall be clothed with shame, and the wicked destroyed."

Job 8:22

"The Lord will defeat your enemies before you; they will march out together against you but scatter before you in seven directions!"

Deuteronomy 28:7

"For the Lord your God is going with you! He will fight for you against your enemies, and he will give you the victory!"

Deuteronomy 20:4

"He will keep you from death in famine, and from the power of the sword in time of war."

Job 5:20

With God's help we shall do mighty things, for he will trample down our foes.

Psalms 60:12

But in that coming day, no weapon turned against you shall succeed, and you will have justice against every courtroom lie. This is the heritage of the servants of the Lord. This is the blessing I have given you, says the Lord.

Isaiah 54:17

The Lord is on my side, he will help me. Let those who hate me beware.

Psalms 118:7

"And by granting us the privilege of serving God fearlessly, freed from our enemies."

Luke 1:74

For the wicked shall not rule the godly, lest the godly be forced to do wrong.

Psalms 125:3

There I'll be when troubles come. He will hide me. He will set me on a high rock out of reach of all my enemies. Then I will bring him sacrifices and sing his praises with much joy.

Psalms 27:5, 6

When a man is trying to please God, God makes even his worst enemies to be at peace with him.

Proverbs 16:7

That is why he is not afraid, but can calmly face his foes.

Psalms 112:8

"Don't you think that God will surely give justice to his people who plead with him day and night?"

Luke 18:7

If any nation comes to fight you, it will not be sent by me to punish you. Therefore it will be routed, for I am on your side.

Isaiah 54:15

The Lord loves those who hate evil; he protects the lives of his people, and rescues them from the wicked.

Psalms 97:10

"But I will deliver you. You shall not be killed by those you fear so much. As a reward for trusting me, I will preserve your life and keep you safe."

Jeremiah 39:17, 18

"You must worship only the Lord; he will save you from all your enemies."

2 Kings 17:39

"Don't be afraid!" Elisha told him. "For our army is bigger than theirs!"

2 Kings 6:16

You need not be afraid of disaster or the plots of wicked men, for the Lord is with you; he protects you.

Proverbs 3:25, 26

See, all your angry enemies lie confused and shattered. Anyone opposing you will die. You will look for them in vain — they will all be gone.

Isaiah 41:11, 12

"He is sending us a Mighty Savior from the royal line of his servant David, just as he promised through his holy prophets long ago — someone to save us from our enemies, from all who hate us."

Luke 1:69–71

"For I am with you and no one can harm you. Many people here in this city belong to me."

Acts 18:10

That is why we can say without any doubt or fear, "The Lord is my Helper and I am not afraid of anything that mere man can do to me."

Hebrews 13:6

Eternal Life

"How earnestly I tell you this — anyone who believes in me already has eternal life."

John 6:47

Jesus told her, "I am the one who raises the dead and gives them life again. Anyone who believes in me, even though he dies like anyone else, shall live again. He is given eternal life for believing in me and shall never perish. Do you believe this, Martha?"

John 11:25, 26

But I am telling you this strange and wonderful secret: we shall not all die, but we shall all be given new bodies! It will all happen in a moment, in the twinkling of an eye, when the last trumpet is blown. For there will be a trumpet blast from the sky and all the Christians who have died will suddenly become alive, with new bodies that will never, never die; and then we who are still alive shall suddenly have new bodies too. For our earthly bodies, the ones we have now that can die, must be transformed into heavenly bodies that cannot perish but will live forever. When this happens, then at last this Scripture will come true — "Death is swallowed up in victory."

1 Corinthians 15:51–54

And he himself has promised us this: eternal life.

1 John 2:25

Death came into the world because of what one man (Adam) did, and it is because of what this other man (Christ) has done that now there is the resurrection from the dead.

1 Corinthians 15:21

I have written this to you who believe in the Son of God so that you may know you have eternal life.

1 John 5:13

"Don't be so surprised! Indeed the time is coming when all the dead in their graves shall hear the voice of God's Son, and shall rise again — those who have done good, to eternal life; and those who have continued in evil, to judgment."

John 5:28, 29

For the Lord himself will come down from heaven with a mighty shout and with the soul-stirring cry of the archangel and the great trumpet-call of God. And the believers who are dead will be the first to rise to meet the Lord.

1 Thessalonians 4:16

"That is why they are here before the throne of God, serving him day and night in his temple. The one sitting on the throne will shelter them; they will never be hungry again, nor thirsty, and they will be fully protected from the scorching noontime heat. For the Lamb standing in front of the throne will feed them and be their Shepherd and lead them to the springs of the Water of Life. And God will wipe their tears away.''

Revelation 7:15–17

''For God loved the world so much that he gave his only Son so that anyone who believes in him shall not perish but have eternal life.''

John 3:16

In the same way, our earthly bodies which die and decay are different from the bodies we shall have when we come back to life again, for they will never die. The bodies we have now embarrass us for they become sick and die; but they will be full of glory when we come back to life again. Yes, they are weak, dying bodies now, but when we live again they will be full of strength. They are just human bodies at death, but when they come back to life they will be superhuman bodies. For just as there are natural, human bodies, there are also super-natural, spiritual bodies.

1 Corinthians 15:42–44

And if the Spirit of God, who raised up Jesus from the dead, lives in you, he will make your dying bodies live again after you die, by means of this same Holy Spirit living within you.

Romans 8:11

"He will wipe away all tears from their eyes, and there shall be no more death, nor sorrow, nor crying, nor pain. All of that has gone forever."

Revelation 21:4

For the wages of sin is death, but the free gift of God is eternal life through Jesus Christ our Lord.

Romans 6:23

"And I know that after this body has decayed, this body shall see God! Then he will be on my side! Yes, I shall see him, not as a stranger, but as a friend! What a glorious hope!"

Job 19:26, 27

If he sows to please his own wrong desires, he will be planting seeds of evil and he will surely reap a harvest of spiritual decay and death; but if he plants the good things of the Spirit, he will reap the everlasting life which the Holy Spirit gives him.

Galatians 6:8

"And many of those whose bodies lie dead and buried will rise up, some to everlasting life and some to shame and everlasting contempt."

Daniel 12:2

Yet we have this assurance: Those who belong to God shall live again. Their bodies shall rise again! Those who dwell in the dust shall awake and sing for joy! For God's light of life will fall like dew upon them!

Isaiah 26:19

For you will not leave me among the dead; you will not allow your beloved one to rot in the grave.

Psalms 16:10

And now he has made all of this plain to us by the coming of our Savior Jesus Christ, who broke the power of death and showed us the way of everlasting life through trusting him.

2 Timothy 1:10

And what is it that God has said? That he has given us eternal life, and that this life is in his Son.

1 John 5:11

For we know that when this tent we live in now is taken down — when we die and leave these bodies — we will have wonderful new bodies in heaven, homes that will be ours forevermore, made for us by God himself, and not by human hands.

2 Corinthians 5:1

"There are many homes up there where my Father lives, and I am going to prepare them for your coming. When everything is ready, then I will come and get you, so that you can always be with me where I am. If this weren't so, I would tell you plainly."

John 14:2, 3

"And this is the will of God, that I should not lose even one of all those he has given me, but that I should raise them to eternal life at the Last Day. For it is my Father's will that everyone who sees his Son and believes on him should have eternal life — that I should raise him at the Last Day."

John 6:39, 40

"And they never die again; in these respects they are like angels, and are sons of God, for they are raised up in new life from the dead."

Luke 20:36

"My sheep recognize my voice, and I know them, and they follow me. I give them eternal life and they shall never perish. No one shall snatch them away from me."

John 10:27, 28

"But anyone who does eat my flesh and drink my blood has eternal life, and I will raise him at the Last Day."

John 6:54

Faith

What is faith? It is the confident assurance that something we want is going to happen. It is the certainty that what we hope for is waiting for us, even though we cannot see it up ahead.

Hebrews 11:1

You can never please God without faith, without depending on him. Anyone who wants to come to God must believe that there is a God and that he rewards those who sincerely look for him.

Hebrews 11:6

If you want to know what God wants you to do, ask him, and he will gladly tell you, for he is always ready to give a bountiful supply of wisdom to all who ask him; he will not resent it. But when you ask him, be sure that you really expect him to tell you, for a doubtful mind will be as unsettled as a wave of the sea that is driven and tossed by the wind.

James 1:5, 6

And now just as you trusted Christ to save you, trust him, too, for each day's problems; live in vital union with him. Let your roots grow down into him and draw up nourishment from him. See that you go on growing in the Lord, and become strong and vigorous in

the truth you were taught. Let your lives overflow with joy and thanksgiving for all he has
done.

Colossians 2:6, 7

Because of his kindness you have been saved
through trusting Christ. And even trusting is
not of yourselves; it too is a gift from God.

Ephesians 2:8

For now we are all children of God through
faith in Jesus Christ.

Galatians 3:26

But you must keep on believing the things
you have be taught. You know they are true for
you know that you can trust those of us who
have taught you. You know how, when you
were a small child, you were taught the holy
Scriptures; and it is these that make you wise to
accept God's salvation by trusting in Christ
Jesus.

2 Timothy 3:14, 15

Keep your eyes open for spiritual danger;
stand true to the Lord; act like men; be strong.
1 Corinthians 16:13

But when the Holy Spirit controls our lives
he will produce this kind of fruit in us: love,
joy, peace, patience, kindness, goodness,
faithfulness.

Galatians 5:22

I have been crucified with Christ: and I myself no longer live, but Christ lives in me. And the real life I now have within this body is a result of my trusting in the Son of God, who loved me and gave himself for me.

Galatians 2:20

We know these things are true by believing, not by seeing.

2 Corinthians 5:7

In reply Jesus said to the disciples, "If you only have faith in God — this is the absolute truth — you can say to this Mount of Olives, 'Rise up and fall into the Mediterranean,' and your command will be obeyed. All that's required is that you really believe and have no doubt!"

Mark 11:22, 23

And I pray that Christ will be more and more at home in your hearts, living within you as you trust in him. May your roots go down deep into the soil of God's marvelous love; and may you be able to feel and understand, as all God's children should, how long, how wide, how deep, and how high his love really is; and to experience this love for yourselves, though it is so great that you will never see the end of it or fully know or understand it. And so at last you will be filled up with God himself.

Ephesians 3:17–19

Since we have such a huge crowd of men of faith watching us from the grandstands, let us strip off anything that slows us down or holds us back, and especially those sins that wrap themselves so tightly around our feet and trip us up; and let us run with patience the particular race that God has set before us. Keep your eyes on Jesus, our leader and instructor. He was willing to die a shameful death on the cross because of the joy he knew would be his afterwards; and now he sits in the place of honor by the throne of God.

Hebrews 12:1, 2

God's Faithfulness

"Understand, therefore, that the Lord your God is the faithful God who for a thousand generations keeps his promises and constantly loves those who love him and who obey his commands."

Deuteronomy 7:9

"God is not a man, that he should lie; He doesn't change his mind like humans do. Has he ever promised, Without doing what he said?"

Numbers 23:19

"For the Lord your God is merciful — he will not abandon you nor destroy you nor forget the promises he has made to your ancestors."

Deuteronomy 4:31

Though a thousand generations pass he never forgets his promise.

Psalms 105:8

Now we can look forward to the salvation God has promised us. There is no longer any room for doubt, and we can tell others that salvation is ours, for there is no question that he will do what he says.

Hebrews 10:23

Even when we are too weak to have any faith left, he remains faithful to us and will help us, for he cannot disown us who are part of himself, and he will always carry out his promises to us.

2 Timothy 2:13

He isn't really being slow about his promised return, even though it sometimes seems that way. But he is waiting, for the good reason that he is not willing that any should perish, and he is giving more time for sinners to repent.

2 Peter 3:9

"Blessed be the Lord who has fulfilled his promise and given rest to his people Israel; not one word has failed of all the wonderful promises proclaimed by his servant Moses."

1 Kings 8:56

O Lord, I will honor and praise your name, for you are my God; you do such wonderful things! You planned them long ago, and now you have accomplished them, just as you said!

Isaiah 25:1

All those who know your mercy, Lord, will count on you for help. For you have never yet forsaken those who trust in you.

Psalms 9:10

There is utter truth in all your laws; your decrees are eternal.

Psalms 119:160

Forever, O Lord, your Word stands firm in heaven. Your faithfulness extends to every generation, like the earth you created.

Psalms 119:89, 90

"And he who is the glory of Israel is not lying, nor will he change his mind, for he is not a man!"

1 Samuel 15:29

He carries out and fulfills all of God's promises, no matter how many of them there are; and we have told everyone how faithful he is, giving glory to his name.

2 Corinthians 1:20

"No, I will not break my covenant; I will not take back one word of what I said."

Psalms 89:34

For the mountains may depart and the hills disappear, but my kindness shall not leave you. My promise of peace for you will never be broken, says the Lord who has mercy upon you.

Isaiah 54:10

"I have said I would do it and I will."

Isaiah 46:11

Fear

And he asked them, "Why were you so fearful? Don't you even yet have confidence in me?"

Mark 4:40

"So don't be afraid, little flock. For it gives your Father great happiness to give you the Kingdom."

Luke 12:32

I am holding you by your right hand — I, the Lord your God — and I say to you, Don't be afraid; I am here to help you.

Isaiah 41:13

"But all who listen to me shall live in peace and safety, unafraid."

Proverbs 1:33

"Don't be afraid of those who can kill only your bodies — but can't touch your souls! Fear only God who can destroy both soul and body in hell."

Matthew 10:28

You need not be afraid of disaster or the plots of wicked men, for the Lord is with you; he protects you.

Proverbs 3:25, 26

For the Holy Spirit, God's gift, does not want you to be afraid of people, but to be wise and strong, and to love them and enjoy being with them.

2 Timothy 1:7

In that wonderful day when the Lord gives his people rest from sorrow and fear, from slavery and chains.

Isaiah 14:3

With them on guard you can sleep without fear.

Proverbs 3:24

For the Lord is watching his children, listening to their prayers; but the Lord's face is hard against those who do evil. Usually no one will hurt you for wanting to do good. But even if they should, you are to be envied, for God will reward you for it.

1 Peter 3:12–14

You will live under a government that is just and fair. Your enemies will stay far away; you will live in peace. Terror shall not come near.

Isaiah 54:14

And so we should not be like cringing, fearful slaves, but we should behave like God's very own children, adopted into the bosom of his family, and calling to him, "Father, Father."

Romans 8:15

That is why we can say without any doubt or fear, "The Lord is my Helper and I am not afraid of anything that mere man can do to me."

Hebrews 13:6

God is our refuge and strength, a tested help in times of trouble.

Psalms 46:1

I, even I, am he who comforts you and gives you all this joy. So what right have you to fear mere mortal men, who wither like the grass and disappear?

Isaiah 51:12

Fear of man is a dangerous trap, but to trust in God means safety.

Proverbs 29:25

He will shield you with his wings! They will shelter you. His faithful promises are your armor. Now you don't need to be afraid of the dark any more, nor fear the dangers of the day; nor dread the plagues of darkness, nor disasters in the morning.

Psalms 91:4–6

Fear not; you will no longer live in shame. The shame of your youth and the sorrows of widowhood will be remembered no more.

Isaiah 54:4

When you go through deep waters and great trouble, I will be with you. When you go through rivers of difficulty, you will not drown! When you walk through the fire of oppression, you will not be burned up — the flames will not consume you.

Isaiah 43:2

"I am leaving you with a gift — peace of mind and heart! And the peace I give isn't fragile like the peace the world gives. So don't be troubled or afraid."

John 14:27

Even when walking through the dark valley of death I will not be afraid, for you are close beside me, guarding, guiding all the way. You provide delicious food for me in the presence of my enemies. You have welcomed me as your guest; blessings overflow!

Psalms 23:4, 5

The Lord is my light and my salvation; whom shall I fear? When evil men come to destroy me, they will stumble and fall! Yes, though a mighty army marches against me, my heart shall know no fear! I am confident that God will save me.

Psalms 27:1–3

But despite all this, overwhelming victory is ours through Christ who loved us enough to die for us. For I am convinced that nothing can ever separate us from his love. Death can't, and life can't. The angels won't, and all the powers of hell itself cannot keep God's love away. Our fears for today, our worries about tomorrow, or where we are — high above the sky, or in the deepest ocean — nothing will ever be able to separate us from the love of God demonstrated by our Lord Jesus Christ when he died for us.

Romans 8:37–39

Food and Clothing

The threshing floors will pile high again with wheat, and the presses overflow with olive oil and wine. And I will give you back the crops the locusts ate! — my great destroying army that I sent against you. Once again you will have all the food you want.

Joel 2:24–26

He sends peace across your nation, and fills your barns with plenty of the finest wheat.

Psalms 147:14

He gives food to those who trust him; he never forgets his promises.

Psalms 111:5

The good man eats to live, while the evil man lives to eat.

Proverbs 13:25

"I will make this city prosperous and satisfy her poor with food."

Psalms 132:15

"So don't worry at all about having enough food and clothing. Why be like the heathen? For they take pride in all these things and are deeply concerned about them. But your heavenly Father already knows perfectly well that you need them, and he will give them to you if you give him first place in your life and live as he wants you to."

Matthew 6:31–33

Forgiveness

"But I say: Love your enemies! Pray for those who persecute you! In that way you will be acting as true sons of your Father in heaven. For he gives his sunlight to both the evil and the good, and sends rain on the just and on the unjust too."

Matthew 5:44, 45

"But when you are praying, first forgive anyone you are holding a grudge against, so that your Father in heaven will forgive you your sins too."

Mark 11:25, 26

"Your heavenly Father will forgive you if you forgive those who sin against you."

Matthew 6:14

Instead, feed your enemy if he is hungry. If he is thirsty give him something to drink....

Romans 12:20

"Love your enemies! Do good to them! Lend to them! And don't be concerned about the fact that they won't repay. Then your reward from heaven will be very great, and you will truly be acting as sons of God: for he is kind to the unthankful and to those who are very wicked. Try to show as much compassion as your Father does. Never criticize or condemn — or it will all come back on you. Go easy on others; then they will do the same for you. For if you give, you will get! Your gift will return to you in full and overflowing measure, pressed down, shaken together to make room for more, and running over. Whatever measure you use to give — large or small — will be used to measure what is given back to you."

Luke 6:35–38

Don't repay evil for evil. Wait for the Lord to handle the matter.

Proverbs 20:22

Fruitfulness

"I am the true Vine, and my Father is the Gardener. He lops off every branch that doesn't produce. And he prunes those branches that bear fruit for even larger crops. He has already tended you by pruning you back for greater strength and usefulness by means of the commands I gave you. Take care to live in me, and let me live in you. For a branch can't produce fruit when severed from the vine. Nor can you be fruitful apart from me. Yes, I am the Vine; you are the branches. Whoever lives in me and I in him shall produce a large crop of fruit. For apart from me you can't do a thing."

John 15:1–5

They are like trees along a river bank bearing luscious fruit each season without fail. Their leaves shall never wither, and all they do shall prosper.

Psalms 1:3

They shall come home and sing songs of joy upon the hills of Zion, and shall be radiant over the goodness of the Lord — the good crops, the wheat and the wine and the oil, and the healthy flocks and herds. Their life shall be like a watered garden, and all their sorrows shall be gone.

Jeremiah 31:12

Even in old age they will still produce fruit and be vital and green.

Psalms 92:14

I will refresh Israel like the dew from heaven; she will blossom as the lily and root deeply in the soil like cedars in Lebanon.

Hosea 14:5

The more you go on in this way, the more you will grow strong spiritually and become fruitful and useful to our Lord Jesus Christ.

2 Peter 1:8

Gossip

"Don't gossip. Don't falsely accuse your neighbor of some crime, for I am Jehovah."

Leviticus 19:16

What dainty morsels rumors are. They are eaten with great relish!

Proverbs 18:8

Don't tell your secrets to a gossip unless you want them broadcast to the world.

Proverbs 20:19

A gossip goes around spreading rumors, while a trustworthy man tries to quiet them.

Proverbs 11:13

An evil man sows strife; gossip separates the best of friends.

Proverbs 16:28

As surely as a wind from the north brings cold, just as surely a retort causes anger!

Proverbs 25:23

Fire goes out for lack of fuel, and tensions disappear when gossip stops. A quarrelsome man starts fights as easily as a match sets fire to paper. Gossip is a dainty morsel eaten with great relish.

Proverbs 26:20–22

Then watch your tongue! Keep your lips from lying.

Psalms 34:13

Growth in Grace

"My true disciples produce bountiful harvests. This brings great glory to my Father."

John 15:8

My prayer for you is that you will overflow more and more with love for others, and at the same time keep on growing in spiritual knowledge and insight.

Philippians 1:9

Dear brothers, giving thanks to God for you is not only the right thing to do, but it is our duty to God, because of the really wonderful way your faith has grown, and because of your growing love for each other.

2 Thessalonians 1:3

Let me add this, dear brothers: You already know how to please God in your daily living, for you know the commands we gave you from the Lord Jesus himself.

1 Thessalonians 4:1

May you always be doing those good, kind things which show that you are a child of God, for this will bring much praise and glory to the Lord.

Philippians 1:11

But to obtain these gifts, you need more than faith; you must also work hard to be good, and even that is not enough. For then you must learn to know God better and discover what he wants you to do.

2 Peter 1:5

"The righteous shall move onward and forward; those with pure hearts shall become stronger and stronger."

Job 17:9

But we Christians have no veil over our faces; we can be mirrors that brightly reflect the glory of the Lord. And as the Spirit of the Lord works within us, we become more and more like him.

2 Corinthians 3:18

The Lord will work out his plans for my life — for your lovingkindness, Lord, continues forever. Don't abandon me — for you made me.

Psalms 138:8

The same Good News that came to you is going out all over the world and changing lives everywhere, just as it changed yours that very first day you heard it and understood about God's great kindness to sinners.

Colossians 1:6

I strain to reach the end of the race and receive the prize for which God is calling us up to heaven because of what Christ Jesus did for us. I hope all of you who are mature Christians will see eye-to-eye with me on these things, and if you disagree on some point, I believe that God will make it plain to you — if you fully obey the truth you have.

Philippians 3:14–16

Guidance

And if you leave God's paths and go astray, you will hear a Voice behind you say, "No, this is the way; walk here."

Isaiah 30:21

For this great God is our God forever and ever. He will be our guide until we die.

Psalms 48:14

We should make plans — counting on God to direct us.

Proverbs 16:9

The steps of good men are directed by the Lord. He delights in each step they take.

Psalms 37:23

He knows just what to do, for God has made him see and understand.

Isaiah 28:26

The upright are directed by their honesty; the wicked shall fall beneath their load of sins.

Proverbs 11:5

In everything you do, put God first, and he will direct you and crown your efforts with success.

Proverbs 3:6

He will bring blind Israel along a path they have not seen before. He will make the darkness bright before them and smooth and straighten out the road ahead. He will not forsake them.

Isaiah 42:16

But even so, you love me! You are holding my right hand! You will keep on guiding me all my life with your wisdom and counsel; and afterwards receive me into the glories of heaven!

Psalms 73:23, 24

I will instruct you (says the Lord) and guide you along the best pathway for your life; I will advise you and watch your progress.

Psalms 32:8

Guilt

But if we confess our sins to him, he can be depended on to forgive us and to cleanse us from every wrong. [And it is perfectly proper for God to do this for us because Christ died to wash away our sins.]

1 John 1:9

Let men cast off their wicked deeds; let them banish from their minds the very thought of doing wrong! Let them turn to the Lord that he may have mercy upon them, and to our God, for he will abundantly pardon!

Isaiah 55:7

". . . For the Lord your God is full of kindness and mercy and will not continue to turn away his face from you if you return to him."

2 Chronicles 30:9

He has removed our sins as far away from us as the east is from the west.

Psalms 103:12

But if we have bad consciences and feel that we have done wrong, the Lord will surely feel it even more, for he knows everything we do.

1 John 3:20

"And I will be merciful to them in their wrongdoings, and I will remember their sins no more."

Hebrews 8:12

At that time it will no longer be necessary to admonish one another to know the Lord. For everyone, both great and small, shall really know me then, says the Lord, and I will forgive and forget their sins.

Jeremiah 31:34

And I will cleanse away all their sins against me, and pardon them.

Jeremiah 33:8

I am writing these things to all of you, my little children, because your sins have been forgiven in the name of Jesus our Savior.

1 John 2:12

But if we are living in the light of God's presence, just as Christ does, then we have wonderful fellowship and joy with each other, and the blood of Jesus his Son cleanses us from every sin.

1 John 1:7

Help in Troubles

The Lord saves the godly! He is their salvation and their refuge when trouble comes.

Psalms 37:39

. . . He is the God who keeps every promise, and gives justice to the poor and oppressed and food to the hungry. He frees the prisoners, and opens the eyes of the blind; he lifts the burdens from those bent down beneath their loads. For the Lord loves good men.

Psalms 146:6-8

The Lord is good. When trouble comes, he is the place to go! And he knows everyone who trusts in him!

Nahum 1:7

If they fall it isn't fatal, for the Lord holds them with his hand.

Psalms 37:24

You are my hiding place from every storm of life; you even keep me from getting into trouble! You surround me with songs of victory.

Psalms 32:7

You have let me sink down deep in desperate problems. But you will bring me back to life again, up from the depths of the earth.

Psalms 71:20

But O my soul, don't be discouraged. Don't be upset. Expect God to act! For I know that I shall again have plenty of reason to praise him for all that he will do. He is my help! He is my God!

Psalms 42:11

My health fails; my spirits droop, yet God remains! He is the strength of my heart; he is mine forever!

Psalms 73:26

How then can evil overtake me or any plague come near? For he orders his angels to protect you wherever you go.

Psalms 91:10, 11

Those who sow tears shall reap joy. Yes, they go out weeping, carrying seed for sowing, and return singing, carrying their sheaves.

Psalms 126:5, 6

Oh, love the Lord, all of you who are his people; for the Lord protects those who are loyal to him, but harshly punishes all who haughtily reject him.

Psalms 31:23

The Lord speaks. The enemy flees. The women at home cry out the happy news: "The armies that came to destroy us have fled!" Now all the women of Israel are dividing the booty. See them sparkle with jewels of silver and gold, covered all over as wings cover doves!

Psalms 68:11–13

"But look! God will not cast away a good man, nor prosper evildoers. He will yet fill your mouth with laughter and your lips with shouts of joy."

Job 8:20, 21

"For he has not despised my cries of deep despair; he has not turned and walked away. When I cried to him, he heard and came."

Psalms 22:24

"He will deliver you again and again, so that no evil can touch you."

Job 5:19

All who are oppressed may come to him. He is a refuge for them in their times of trouble.

Psalms 9:9

Though I am surrounded by troubles, you will bring me safely through them. You will clench your fist against my angry enemies! Your power will save me.

Psalms 138:7

You have turned on my light! The Lord my God has made my darkness turn to light.

Psalms 18:28

The good man does not escape all troubles — he has them too. But the Lord helps him in each and every one.

Psalms 34:19

For the Lord will not abandon him forever. Although God gives him grief, yet he will show compassion too, according to the greatness of his lovingkindness. For he does not enjoy afflicting men and causing sorrow.

Lamentations 3:31–33

The Lord is my fort where I can enter and be safe; no one can follow me in and slay me. He is a rugged mountain where I hide; he is my Savior, a rock where none can reach me, and a tower of safety. He is my shield. He is like the strong horn of a mighty fighting bull.

Psalms 18:2

Do not rejoice against me, O my enemy, for though I fall, I will rise again! When I sit in darkness, the Lord himself will be my Light. I will be patient while the Lord punishes me, for I have sinned against him; then he will defend me from my enemies, and punish them for all the evil they have done to me. God will bring me out of my darkness into the light, and I will see his goodness.

Michah 7:8, 9

"I have told you all this so that you will have peace of heart and mind. Here on earth you will have many trials and sorrows; but cheer up, for I have overcome the world."

John 16:33

Holy Spirit

"Come here and listen to me! I'll pour out the spirit of wisdom upon you, and make you wise."

Proverbs 1:23

"And I will ask the Father and he will give you another Comforter, and he will never leave you. He is the Holy Spirit, the Spirit who leads into all truth. The world at large cannot receive him, for it isn't looking for him and doesn't recognize him. But you do, for he lives with you now and some day shall be in you."

John 14:16, 17

"For the Scriptures declare that rivers of living water shall flow from the inmost being of anyone who believes in me." (He was speaking of the Holy Spirit, who would be given to everyone believing in him; but the Spirit had not yet been given, because Jesus had not yet returned to his glory in heaven.)

John 7:38, 39

"When the Holy Spirit, who is truth, comes, he shall guide you into all truth, for he will not be presenting his own ideas, but will be passing on to you what he has heard. He will tell you about the future."

John 16:13

"As for me, this is my promise to them," says the Lord: "My Holy Spirit shall not leave them, and they shall want the good and hate the wrong — they and their children and their children's children forever."

Isaiah 59:21

"And if even sinful persons like yourselves give children what they need, don't you realize that your heavenly Father will do at least as much, and give the Holy Spirit to those who ask for him?"

Luke 11:13

"But the water I give them," he said, "becomes a perpetual spring within them, watering them forever with eternal life."

John 4:14

"And I will put my Spirit within you so that you will obey my laws and do whatever I command."

Ezekiel 36:27

Now God can bless the Gentiles, too, with this same blessing he promised to Abraham; and all of us as Christians can have the promised Holy Spirit through this faith.

Galatians 3:14

But you have received the Holy Spirit and he lives within you, in your hearts, so that you don't need anyone to teach you what is right. For he teaches you all things, and he is the

Truth, and no liar; and so, just as he has said, you must live in Christ, never to depart from him.

1 John 2:27

And in the same way — by our faith — the Holy Spirit helps us with our daily problems and in our praying. For we don't even know what we should pray for, nor how to pray as we should; but the Holy Spirit prays for us with such feeling that it cannot be expressed in words. And the Father who knows all hearts knows, of course, what the Spirit is saying as he pleads for us in harmony with God's own will.

Romans 8:26, 27

For, after all, the important thing for us as Christians is not what we eat or drink but stirring up goodness and peace and joy from the Holy Spirit.

Romans 14:17

And God has actually given us his Spirit (not the world's spirit) to tell us about the wonderful free gifts of grace and blessing that God has given us.

1 Corinthians 2:12

And so we should not be like cringing, fearful slaves, but we should behave like God's very own children, adopted into the bosom of his family, and calling to him, "Father, Father."

Romans 8:15

Honesty

"You must not steal nor lie nor defraud."

Leviticus 19:11

For your sins are very great — is there to be no end of getting rich by cheating? The homes of the wicked are full of ungodly treasures and lying scales. Shall I say "Good!" to all your merchants with their bags of false, deceitful weights? How could God be just while saying that? Your rich men are wealthy through extortion and violence; your citizens are so used to lying that their tongues can't tell the truth!

Micah 6:10–12

"You must be impartial in judgment. Use accurate measurements — lengths, weights, and volumes — and give full measure."

Leviticus 19:35

The Lord hates cheating and delights in honesty.

Proverbs 11:1

"In all your transactions you must use accurate scales and honest measurements, so that you will have a long, good life in the land the Lord your God is giving you. All who cheat with unjust weights and measurements are detestable to the Lord your God."

Deuteronomy 25:13–16

And this also is God's will: that you never cheat in this matter by taking another man's wife, because the Lord will punish you terribly for this, as we have solemnly told you before. For God has not called us to be dirty-minded and full of lust, but to be holy and clean.

1 Thessalonians 4:6, 7

Don't tell lies to each other; it was your old life with all its wickedness that did that sort of thing; now it is dead and gone. You are living a brand new kind of life that is continually learning more and more of what is right, and trying constantly to be more and more like Christ who created this new life within you.

Colossians 3:9, 10

Evil men borrow and "cannot pay it back"! But the good man returns what he owes with some extra besides.

Psalms 37:21

Don't withhold repayment of your debts. Don't say "some other time," if you can pay now.

Proverbs 3:27, 28

"You must fear your God and not overcharge! For I am Jehovah."

Leviticus 25:17

A little, gained honestly, is better than great wealth gotten by dishonest means.

Proverbs 16:8

I will tell you who can live here: All who are honest and fair, who reject making profit by fraud, who hold back their hands from taking bribes, who refuse to listen to those who plot murder, who shut their eyes to all enticement to do wrong. Such as these shall dwell on high. The rocks of the mountains will be their fortress of safety; food will be supplied to them and they will have all the water they need.

Isaiah 33:15, 16

Hope

But O my soul, don't be discouraged. Don't be upset. Expect God to act! For I know that I shall again have plenty of reason to praise him for all that he will do. He is my help! He is my God!

Psalms 42:11

Because of this, your trust can be in God who raised Christ from the dead and gave him great glory. Now your faith and hope can rest in him alone.

1 Peter 1:21

So now you can look forward soberly and intelligently to more of God's kindness to you when Jesus Christ returns.

1 Peter 1:13

And everyone who really believes this will try to stay pure because Christ is pure.

1 John 3:3

The godly have a refuge when they die, but the wicked are crushed by their sins.

Proverbs 14:32

And you are looking forward to the joys of heaven, and have been ever since the Gospel first was preached to you.

Colossians 1:5

He has kept this secret for centuries and generations past, but now at last it has pleased him to tell it to those who love him and live for him, and the riches and glory of his plan are for you Gentiles too. And this is the secret: that Christ in your hearts is your only hope of glory.

Colossians 1:26, 27

So cheer up! Take courage if you are depending on the Lord.

Psalms 31:24

O Lord, you alone are my hope; I've trusted you from childhood.

Psalms 71:5

All honor to God, the God and Father of our Lord Jesus Christ; for it is his boundless mercy that has given us the privilege of being born again, so that we are now members of God's own family. Now we live in the hope of eternal life because Christ rose again from the dead.

1 Peter 1:3

Hospitality

Cheerfully share your home with those who need a meal or a place to stay for the night. God has given each of you some special abilities; be sure to use them to help each other, passing on to others God's many kinds of blessings.

1 Peter 4:9, 10

If you have a friend who is in need of food and clothing, and you say to him, "Well, good-bye and God bless you; stay warm and eat hearty," and then don't give him clothes or food, what good does that do?

James 2:15, 16

"If anyone so much as gives you a cup of water because you are Christ's — I say this solemnly — he won't lose his reward."

Mark 9:41

"And I was a constant example to you in helping the poor; for I remembered the words of the Lord Jesus, 'It is more blessed to give than to receive.' "

Acts 20:35

But if someone who is supposed to be a Christian has money enough to live well, and sees a brother in need, and won't help him — how can God's love be within him?

1 John 3:17

Of course, I don't mean that those who receive your gifts should have an easy time of it at your expense, but you should divide with them. Right now you have plenty and can help them; then at some other time they can share with you when you need it. In this way each will have as much as he needs.

2 Corinthians 8:13, 14

When God's children are in need, you be the one to help them out. And get into the habit of inviting guests home for dinner or, if they need lodging, for the night.

Romans 12:13

" 'For I was hungry and you fed me; I was thirsty and you gave me water; I was a stranger and you invited me into your homes; naked and you clothed me; sick and in prison, and you visited me.' "

Matthew 25:35, 36

"And I, the King, will tell them, 'When you did it to these my brothers you were doing it to me.' "

Matthew 25:40

Don't forget to be kind to strangers, for some who have done this have entertained angels without realizing it!

Hebrews 13:2

Humility

"Therefore anyone who humbles himself as this little child, is the greatest in the Kingdom of Heaven."

Matthew 18:4

Lord, you know the hopes of humble people. Surely you will hear their cries and comfort their hearts by helping them.

Psalms 10:17

"But those who think themselves great shall be disappointed and humbled; and those who humble themselves shall be exalted."

Matthew 23:12

"If you are attacked and knocked down, you will know that there is someone who will lift you up again. Yes, he will save the humble."

Job 22:29

Better poor and humble than proud and rich.

Proverbs 16:19

The Lord mocks at mockers, but helps the humble.

Proverbs 3:34

True humility and respect for the Lord lead a man to riches, honor and long life.

Proverbs 22:4

Humility and reverence for the Lord will make you both wise and honored.

Proverbs 15:33

Pride ends in a fall, while humility brings honor.

Proverbs 29:23

If you will humble yourselves under the mighty hand of God, in his good time he will lift you up.

1 Peter 5:6

Jealousy

" 'You must not burn with desire for another man's wife, nor envy him for his home, land, servants, oxen, donkeys, nor anything else he owns.' "

Deuteronomy 5:21

For wherever there is jealousy or selfish ambition, there will be disorder and every other kind of evil.

James 3:16

Or what do you think the Scripture means when it says that the Holy Spirit, whom God has placed within us, watches over us with tender jealousy?

James 4:5

Rest in the Lord; wait patiently for him to act. Don't be envious of evil men who prosper.

Psalms 37:7

For these men brag of all their evil lusts; they revile God and congratulate those the Lord abhors, whose only goal in life is money.

Psalms 10:3

Don't envy violent men. Don't copy their ways.

Proverbs 3:31

A relaxed attitude lengthens a man's life; jealousy rots it away.

Proverbs 14:30

Jealousy is more dangerous and cruel than anger.

Proverbs 27:4

Then I observed that the basic motive for success is the driving force of envy and jealousy! But this, too, is foolishness, chasing the wind.

Ecclesiastes 4:4

If we are living now by the Holy Spirit's power, let us follow the Holy Spirit's leading in every part of our lives. Then we won't need to look for honors and popularity, which lead to jealousy and hard feelings.

Galatians 5:25, 26

Don't envy godless men; don't even enjoy their company.

Proverbs 24:1

And by all means don't brag about being wise and good if you are bitter and jealous and selfish; that is the worst sort of lie.

James 3:14

Don't envy evil men but continue to reverence the Lord all the time, for surely you have a wonderful future ahead of you. There is hope for you yet!

Proverbs 23:17, 18

Don't think only of yourself. Try to think of the other fellow, too, and what is best for him.

1 Corinthians 10:24

Then turning to his disciples he said, "Don't worry about whether you have enough food to eat or clothes to wear. For life consists of far more than food and clothes."

Luke 12:22, 23

Joy

You will live in joy and peace. The mountains and hills, the trees of the field — all the world around you — will rejoice.

Isaiah 55:12

Blessed are those who hear the joyful blast of the trumpet, for they shall walk in the light of your presence. They rejoice all day long in your wonderful reputation and in your perfect righteousness.

Psalms 89:15, 16

Songs of joy at the news of our rescue are sung in the homes of the godly. The strong arm of the Lord has done glorious things!

Psalms 118:15, 16

Yes, the gladness you have given me is far greater than their joys at harvest time as they gaze at their bountiful crops.

Psalms 4:7

Those who sow tears shall reap joy. Yes, they go out weeping, carrying seed for sowing, and return singing, carrying their sheaves.

Psalms 126:5, 6

Light is sown for the godly and joy for the good. May all who are godly be happy in the Lord and crown him, our holy God.

Psalms 97:11, 12

"Then you will delight yourself in the Lord, and look up to God."

Job 22:26

"I have told you this so that you will be filled with my joy. Yes, your cup of joy will overflow!"

John 15:11

Yet I will rejoice in the Lord; I will be happy in the God of my salvation.

Habakkuk 3:18

The time will come when God's redeemed will all come home again. They shall come with singing to Jerusalem, filled with joy and everlasting gladness; sorrow and mourning will all disappear.

Isaiah 51:11

No wonder we are happy in the Lord! For we are trusting him. We trust his holy name.

Psalms 33:21

You love him even though you have never seen him; though not seeing him, you trust him; and even now you are happy with the inexpressible joy that comes from heaven itself.

1 Peter 1:8

Let me tell you how happy God has made me! For he has clothed me with garments of salvation and draped about me the robe of righteousness. I am like a bridegroom in his wedding suit or a bride with her jewels.

Isaiah 61:10

"It is a time to celebrate with a hearty meal, and to send presents to those in need, for the joy of the Lord is your strength. You must not be dejected and sad!"

Nehemiah 8:10

And the joy of the Lord shall fill you full; you shall glory in the God of Israel.

Isaiah 41:16

And the godly shall rejoice in the Lord, and trust and praise him.

Psalms 64:10

At last I shall be fully satisfied; I will praise you with great joy.

Psalms 63:5

But may the godly man exult. May he rejoice and be merry.

Psalms 68:3

"You have sorrow now, but I will see you again and then you will rejoice; and no one can rob you of that joy."

John 16:22

Laziness

This should be your ambition: to live a quiet life, minding your own business and doing your own work, just as we told you before. As a result, people who are not Christians will trust and respect you, and you will not need to depend on others for enough money to pay your bills.

1 Thessalonians 4:11, 12

Never be lazy in your work but serve the Lord enthusiastically.

Romans 12:11

Hard work brings prosperity; playing around brings poverty.

Proverbs 28:19

Lazy men are soon poor; hard workers get rich. A wise youth makes hay while the sun shines, but what a shame to see a lad who sleeps away his hour of opportunity.

Proverbs 10:4, 5

Even while we were still there with you we gave you this rule: "He who does not work shall not eat." Yet we hear that some of you are living in laziness, refusing to work, and wasting your time in gossiping. In the name of the Lord Jesus Christ we appeal to such people — we command them — to quiet down, get to work, and earn their own living.

2 Thessalonians 3:10–12

Work hard, like a farmer who gets paid well if he raises a large crop.

2 Timothy 2:6

If anyone is stealing he must stop it and begin using those hands of his for honest work so he can give to others in need.

Ephesians 4:28

I walked by the field of a certain lazy fellow and saw that it was overgrown with thorns, and covered with weeds; and its walls were broken down. Then, as I looked, I learned this lesson:
"A little extra sleep,
A little more slumber,
A little folding of the hands to rest"
means that poverty will break in upon you suddenly like a robber, and violently like a bandit.

Proverbs 24:30–34

If you love sleep, you will end in poverty. Stay awake, work hard, and there will be plenty to eat!

Proverbs 20:13

A lazy fellow has trouble all through life; the good man's path is easy!

Proverbs 15:19

Steady plodding brings prosperity; hasty speculation brings poverty.

Proverbs 21:5

Hard work means prosperity; only a fool idles away his time.

Proverbs 12:24

Riches can disappear fast. And the king's crown doesn't stay in his family forever — so watch your business interests closely.

Proverbs 27:23

Know the state of your flocks and your herds; then there will be lamb's wool enough for clothing, and goat's milk enough for food for all your household after the hay is harvested, and the new crop appears, and the mountain grasses are gathered in.

Proverbs 27:24–27

Well, one thing, at least, is good: it is for a man to eat well, drink a good glass of wine, accept his position in life, and enjoy his work whatever his job may be, for however long the Lord may let him live. And, of course, it is very good if a man has received wealth from the Lord, and the good health to enjoy it. To enjoy your work and to accept your lot in life — that is indeed a gift from God.

Ecclesiastes 5:18, 19

Loneliness

"No, I will not abandon you or leave you as orphans in the storm — I will come to you."

John 14:18

Then, when you call, the Lord will answer. "Yes, I am here," he will quickly reply. . . .

Isaiah 58:9

Others died that you might live; I traded their lives for yours because you are precious to me and honored, and I love you.

Isaiah 43:4

"And be a Father to you, and you will be my sons and daughters."

2 Corinthians 6:18

"What's more, I am with you, and will protect you wherever you go, and will bring you back safely to this land: I will be with you constantly until I have finished giving you all I am promising."

Genesis 28:15

So you have everything when you have Christ, and you are filled with God through your union with Christ. He is the highest Ruler, with authority over every other power.

Colossians 2:10

I am poor and needy, yet the Lord is thinking about me right now! O my God, you are my helper. You are my Savior; come quickly, and save me. Please don't delay!

Psalms 40:17

Long Life

"I will be your God through all your lifetime, yes, even when your hair is white with age. I made you and I will care for you. I will carry you along and be your Savior."

Isaiah 46:4

"And as you say, older men like me are wise. They understand. But true wisdom and power are God's. He alone knows what we should do; he understands."

Job 12:12, 13

The glory of young men is their strength; of old men, their experience.

Proverbs 20:29

An old man's grandchildren are his crowning glory. A child's glory is his father.

Proverbs 17:6

"You shall live a long, good life; like standing grain, you'll not be harvested until it's time!"

Job 5:26

"And your life will be cloudless; any darkness will be as bright as morning!"

Job 11:17

But as for you, speak up for the right living that goes along with true Christianity. Teach the older men to be serious and unruffled;

they must be sensible, knowing and believing the truth and doing everything with love and patience. Teach the older women to be quiet and respectful in everything they do. They must not go around speaking evil of others and must not be heavy drinkers, but they should be teachers of goodness. These older women must train the younger women to live quietly, to love their husbands and their children, and to be sensible and clean minded, spending their time in their own homes, being kind and obedient to their husbands, so that the Christian faith can't be spoken against by those who know them.

Titus 2:1–5

O God, you have helped me from my earliest childhood — and I have constantly testified to others of the wonderful things you do. And now that I am old and gray, don't forsake me. Give me time to tell this new generation (and their children too) about all your mighty miracles.

Psalms 71:17, 18

And now, in my old age, don't set me aside. Don't forsake me now when my strength is failing.

Psalms 71:9

Lord, help me to realize how brief my time on earth will be. Help me to know that I am here for but a moment more. My life is no longer than my hand! My whole lifetime is but a moment to you.

Psalms 39:4, 5

So Moses told the people, "You must obey all the commandments of the Lord your God, following his directions in every detail, going the whole way he has laid out for you; only then will you live long and prosperous lives in the land you are to enter and possess."

Deuteronomy 5:32, 33

My son, never forget the things I've taught you. If you want a long and satisfying life, closely follow my instructions.

Proverbs 3:1, 2

"The purpose of these laws is to cause you, your sons, and your grandsons to reverence the Lord your God by obeying all of his instructions as long as you live; if you do, you will have long, prosperous years ahead of you."

Deuteronomy 6:2

"I will satisfy him with a full life and give him my salvation."

Psalms 91:16

Reverence for God adds hours to each day; so how can the wicked expect a long, good life?

Proverbs 10:27

"I, Wisdom, will make the hours of your day more profitable and the years of your life more fruitful."

Proverbs 9:11

Brotherly Love

"And so I am giving a new commandment to you now — love each other just as much as I love you. Your strong love for each other will prove to the world that you are my disciples."

John 13:34, 35

Don't just pretend that you love others: really love them. Hate what is wrong. Stand on the side of the good. Love each other with brotherly affection and take delight in honoring each other.

Romans 12:9, 10

But concerning the pure brotherly love that there should be among God's people, I don't need to say very much, I'm sure! For God himself is teaching you to love one another.

1 Thessalonians 4:9

But whoever loves his fellow man is "walking in the light" and can see his way without stumbling around in darkness and sin.

1 John 2:10

Now you can have real love for everyone because your souls have been cleansed from selfishness and hatred when you trusted Christ to save you; so see to it that you really do love each other warmly, with all your hearts.

1 Peter 1:22

Dear friends, let us practice loving each other, for love comes from God and those who are loving and kind show that they are the children of God, and that they are getting to know him better. But if a person isn't loving and kind, it shows that he doesn't know God — for God is love.

1 John 4:7, 8

Little children, let us stop just saying we love people; let us really love them, and show it by our actions.

1 John 3:18

Dear friends, since God loved us as much as that, we surely ought to love each other too.

1 John 4:11

Since you have been chosen by God who has given you this new kind of life, and because of his deep love and concern for you, you should practice tenderhearted mercy and kindness to others. Don't worry about making a good impression on them but be ready to suffer quietly and patiently. Be gentle and ready to forgive; never hold grudges. Remember, the Lord forgave you, so you must forgive others.

Colossians 3:12, 13

God's Love

"For God loved the world so much that he gave his only Son so that anyone who believes in him shall not perish but have eternal life."

John 3:16

"And he will love you and bless you and make you into a great nation. He will make you fertile and give fertility to your ground and to your animals, so that you will have large crops of grain, grapes, and olives, and great flocks of cattle, sheep, and goats when you arrive in the land he promised your fathers to give you."

Deuteronomy 7:13

. . . He frees the prisoners, and opens the eyes of the blind; he lifts the burdens from those bent down beneath their loads. For the Lord loves good men.

Psalms 146:7, 8

The Lord despises the deeds of the wicked, but loves those who try to be good.

Proverbs 15:9

Your children will care for you, O Jerusalem, with joy like that of a young man who marries a virgin; and God will rejoice over you as a bridegroom with his bride.

Isaiah 62:5

"For the Lord your God has arrived to live among you. He is a mighty Savior. He will give you victory. He will rejoice over you in great gladness; he will love you and not accuse you." Is that a joyous choir I hear? No, it is the Lord himself exulting over you in happy song.

Zephaniah 3:17

For long ago the Lord had said to Israel: I have loved you, O my people, with an everlasting love; with lovingkindness I have drawn you to me.

Jeremiah 31:3

Then I will cure you of idolatry and faithlessness, and my love will know no bounds, for my anger will be forever gone!

Hosea 14:4

I will rejoice to do them good and will replant them in this land, with great joy.

Jeremiah 32:41

But God is so rich in mercy; he loved us so much that even though we were spiritually dead and doomed by our sins, he gave us back our lives again when he raised Christ from the dead — only by his undeserved favor have we ever been saved — and lifted us up from the grave into glory along with Christ, where we sit with him in the heavenly realms — all because of what Christ Jesus did. And now God can always point to us as examples of how very,

very rich his kindness is, as shown in all he has done for us through Jesus Christ.

Ephesians 2:4–7

In this act we see what real love is: it is not our love for God, but his love for us when he sent his Son to satisfy God's anger against our sins.

1 John 4:10

We know how much God loves us because we have felt his love and because we believe him when he tells us that he loves us dearly. God is love, and anyone who lives in love is living with God and God is living in him.

1 John 4:16

So you see, our love for him comes as a result of his loving us first.

1 John 4:19

"And I have revealed you to them, and will keep on revealing you so that the mighty love you have for me may be in them, and I in them."

John 17:26

"I in them and you in me, all being perfected into one — so that the world will know you sent me and will understand that you love them as much as you love me."

John 17:23

"For the Father himself loves you dearly because you love me and believe that I came from the Father."

John 16:27

May our Lord Jesus Christ himself and God our Father, who has loved us and given us everlasting comfort and hope which we don't deserve, comfort your hearts with all comfort, and help you in every good thing you say and do.

2 Thessalonians 2:16, 17

Loving God

"Understand, therefore, that the Lord your God is the faithful God who for a thousand generations keeps his promises and constantly loves those who love him and who obey his commands."

Deuteronomy 7:9

"I love all who love me. Those who search for me shall surely find me."

Proverbs 8:17

"The one who obeys me is the one who loves me; and because he loves me, my Father will love him; and I will too, and I will reveal myself to him."

John 14:21

"Those who love and follow me are indeed wealthy. I fill their treasuries."

Proverbs 8:21

Be delighted with the Lord. Then he will give you all your heart's desires.

Psalms 37:4

He protects all those who love him, but destroys the wicked.

Psalms 145:20

For the Lord says, "Because he loves me, I will rescue him; I will make him great because he trusts in my name."

Psalms 91:14

That is what is meant by the Scriptures which say that no mere man has ever seen, heard or even imagined what wonderful things God has ready for those who love the Lord.

1 Corinthians 2:9

"And if you will carefully obey all of his commandments that I am going to give you today, and if you will love the Lord your God with all your hearts and souls, and will worship him, then he will continue to send both the early and late rains that will produce wonderful crops of grain, grapes for your wine, and olive oil. He will give you lush pastureland for your cattle to graze in, and you yourselves shall have plenty to eat and be fully content."

Deuteronomy 11:13–15

May God's grace and blessing be upon all who sincerely love our Lord Jesus Christ.

Ephesians 6:24

Lust

What is causing the quarrels and fights among you? Isn't it because there is a whole army of evil desires within you? You want what you don't have, so you kill to get it. You long for what others have, and can't afford it, so you start a fight to take it away from them. And yet the reason you don't have what you want is that you don't ask God for it. And even when you do ask you don't get it because your whole aim is wrong — you want only what will give you pleasure. You are like an unfaithful wife who loves her husband's enemies. Don't you realize that making friends with God's enemies — the evil pleasures of this world — makes you an enemy of God? I say it again, that if your aim is to enjoy the evil pleasure of the unsaved world, you cannot also be a friend of God.

James 4:1–4

For all these worldly things, these evil desires — the craze for sex, the ambition to buy everything that appeals to you, and the pride that comes from wealth and importance — these are not from God. They are from this evil world itself. And this world is fading away, and these evil, forbidden things will go with it, but whoever keeps doing the will of God will live forever.

1 John 2:16, 17

"The laws of Moses said, 'You shall not commit adultery.' But I say: Anyone who even looks at a woman with lust in his eye has already committed adultery with her in his heart."

Matthew 5:27, 28

Don't lust for their beauty. Don't let their coyness seduce you. For a prostitute will bring a man to poverty, and an adulteress may cost him his very life. Can a man hold fire against his chest and not be burned? Can he walk on hot coals and not blister his feet? So it is with the man who commits adultery with another's wife. He shall not go unpunished for this sin.

Proverbs 6:25–29

So give yourselves humbly to God. Resist the devil and he will flee from you. And when you draw close to God, God will draw close to you. Wash your hands, you sinners, and let your hearts be filled with God alone to make them pure and true to him.

James 4:7, 8

Dear brothers, you are only visitors here. Since your real home is in heaven I beg you to keep away from the evil pleasures of this world; they are not for you, for they fight against your very souls.

1 Peter 2:11

Obey God because you are his children; don't slip back into your old ways — doing evil because you knew no better. But be holy now in everything you do, just as the Lord is holy, who invited you to be his child. He himself has said, "You must be holy, for I am holy."

1 Peter 1:14–16

Run from anything that gives you the evil thoughts that young men often have, but stay close to anything that makes you want to do right. Have faith and love, and enjoy the companionship of those who love the Lord and have pure hearts.

2 Timothy 2:22

Once we, too, were foolish and disobedient; we were misled by others and became slaves to many evil pleasures and wicked desires. Our lives were full of resentment and envy. We hated others and they hated us. But when the time came for the kindness and love of God our Savior to appear, then he saved us — not because we were good enough to be saved, but because of his kindness and pity — by washing away our sins and giving us the new joy of the indwelling Holy Spirit.

Titus 3:3–5

All of us used to be just as they are, our lives expressing the evil within us, doing every wicked thing that our passions or our evil thoughts might lead us into. We started out bad, being born with evil natures, and were under God's anger just like everyone else. But God is so rich in mercy; he loved us so much that even though we were spiritually dead and doomed by our sins, he gave us back our lives again when he raised Christ from the dead — only by his un-deserved favor have we ever been saved — and lifted us up from the grave into glory along with Christ, where we sit with him in the heavenly realms — all because of what Christ Jesus did.

Ephesians 2:3–6

For the free gift of eternal salvation is now being offered to everyone; and along with this gift comes the realization that God wants us to turn from godless living and sinful pleasures and to live good, God-fearing lives day after day.

Titus 2:11, 12

Those who belong to Christ have nailed their natural evil desires to his cross and crucified them there.

Galatians 5:24

And remember, when someone wants to do wrong it is never God who is tempting him, for God never wants to do wrong and never tempts anyone else to do it.

James 1:13

That in the last times there would come these scoffers whose whole purpose in life is to enjoy themselves in every evil way imaginable. They stir up arguments; they love the evil things of the world; they do not have the Holy Spirit living in them. But you, dear friends, must build up your lives ever more strongly upon the foundation of our holy faith, learning to pray in the power and strength of the Holy Spirit. Stay always within the boundaries where God's love can reach and bless you. Wait patiently for the eternal life that our Lord Jesus Christ in his mercy is going to give you.

Jude 18–21

I advise you to obey only the Holy Spirit's instructions. He will tell you where to go and what to do, and then you won't always be doing the wrong things your evil nature wants you to. For we naturally love to do evil things that are just the opposite from the things that the Holy Spirit tells us to do; and the good things we want to do when the Spirit has his way with us are just the opposite of our natural desires. These two forces within us are constantly fighting each other to win control over us, and our wishes are never free from their pressures.

Galatians 5:16, 17

So look upon your old sin nature as dead and unresponsive to sin, and instead be alive to God, alert to him, through Jesus Christ our Lord. Do not let sin control your puny body any longer; do not give in to its sinful desires. Sin need never again be your master, for now you are no longer tied to the law where sin enslaves you, but you are free under God's favor and mercy.

Romans 6:11, 12, 14

And by that same mighty power he has given us all the other rich and wonderful blessings he promised; for instance, the promise to save us from the lust and rottenness all around us, and to give us his own character.

2 Peter 1:4

Lying

Don't tell lies to each other; it was your old life with all its wickedness that did that sort of thing; now it is dead and gone. You are living a brand new kind of life that is continually learning more and more of what is right, and trying constantly to be more and more like Christ who created this new life within you.

Colossians 3:9, 10

"You must not steal nor lie nor defraud. You must not swear to a falsehood, thus bringing reproach upon the name of your God, for I am Jehovah."

Leviticus 19:11, 12

Telling lies about someone is as harmful as hitting him with an axe, or wounding him with a sword, or shooting him with a sharp arrow.

Proverbs 25:18

"Don't plot harm to others; don't swear that something is true when it isn't! How I hate all that sort of thing!" says the Lord.

Zechariah 8:17

A truthful witness never lies; a false witness always lies.

Proverbs 14:5

"How many times must I tell you to speak only what the Lord tells you to?" the king demanded.

1 Kings 22:16

Punish false witnesses. Track down liars.

Proverbs 19:5

"If anyone gives false witness, claiming he has seen someone do wrong when he hasn't, both men shall be brought before the priests and judges on duty before the Lord at the time. They must be closely questioned, and if the witness is lying, his penalty shall be the punishment he thought the other man would get. In this way you will purge out evil from among you."

Deuteronomy 19:16–19

"But cowards who turn back from following me, and those who are unfaithful to me, and the corrupt, and murderers, and the immoral, and those conversing with demons, and idol worshipers and all liars — their doom is in the Lake that burns with fire and sulphur. This is the Second Death."

Revelation 21:8

A false witness shall be punished and a liar shall be caught.

Proverbs 19:9

Don't testify spitefully against an innocent neighbor. Why lie about him?

Proverbs 24:28

These men are born sinners, lying from their earliest words!

Psalms 58:3

"Do not pass along untrue reports. Do not cooperate with an evil man by affirming on the witness stand something you know is false."

Exodus 23:1

And by all means don't brag about being wise and good if you are bitter and jealous and selfish; that is the worst sort of lie.

James 3:14

Trust stands the test of time; lies are soon exposed.

Proverbs 12:19

Marriage

Live happily with the woman you love through the fleeting days of life, for the wife God gives you is your best reward down here for all your earthly toil.

Ecclesiastes 9:9

Drink from your own well, my son — be faithful and true to your wife.

Proverbs 5:15

Let your manhood be a blessing; rejoice in the wife of your youth. Let her charms and tender embrace satisfy you. Let her love alone fill you with delight. Why delight yourself with prostitutes, embracing what isn't yours?

Proverbs 5:18–20

The man should give his wife all that is her right as a married woman, and the wife should do the same for her husband.

1 Corinthians 7:3

You wives must submit to your husbands' leadership in the same way you submit to the Lord. For a husband is in charge of his wife in the same way Christ is in charge of his body the church. (He gave his very life to take care of it and be its Savior!)

Ephesians 5:22, 23

And you husbands, show the same kind of love to your wives as Christ showed to the church when he died for her.

Ephesians 5:25

That is how husbands should treat their wives, loving them as parts of themselves. For since a man and his wife are now one, a man is really doing himself a favor and loving himself when he loves his wife!

Ephesians 5:28

(That the husband and wife are one body is proved by the Scripture which says, "A man must leave his father and mother when he marries, so that he can be perfectly joined to his wife, and the two shall be one.")

Ephesians 5:31

So again I say, a man must love his wife as a part of himself; and the wife must see to it that she deeply respects her husband — obeying, praising and honoring him.

Ephesians 5:33

But anyone who won't care for his own relatives when they need help, especially those living in his own family, has no right to say he is a Christian. Such a person is worse than the heathen.

1 Timothy 5:8

You wives, submit yourselves to your husbands, for that is what the Lord has planned for you. And you husbands must be loving and kind to your wives and not bitter against them, nor harsh.

Colossians 3:18, 19

You husbands must be careful of your wives, being thoughtful of their needs and honoring them as the weaker sex. Remember that you and your wife are partners in receiving God's blessings, and if you don't treat her as you should, your prayers will not get ready answers.

1 Peter 3:7

These older women must train the younger women to live quietly, to love their husbands and their children, and to be sensible and clean minded, spending their time in their own homes, being kind and obedient to their husbands, so that the Christian faith can't be spoken against by those who know them.

Titus 2:4, 5

Meekness

"The meek and lowly are fortunate! for the whole wide world belongs to them."

Matthew 5:5

His delight will be obedience to the Lord. He will not judge by appearance, false evidence, or hearsay, but will defend the poor and the exploited. He will rule against the wicked who oppress them.

Isaiah 11:3, 4

The poor shall eat and be satisfied; all who seek the Lord shall find him and shall praise his name. Their hearts shall rejoice with everlasting joy.

Psalms 22:26

For Jehovah enjoys his people; he will save the humble.

Psalms 149:4

The meek will be filled with fresh joy from the Lord, and the poor shall exult in the Holy One of Israel.

Isaiah 29:19

The Lord supports the humble, but brings the wicked into the dust.

Psalms 147:6

He will teach the ways that are right and best to those who humbly turn to him.

Psalms 25:9

Beg him to save you, all who are humble —
all who have tried to obey.

Zephaniah 2:3

Be beautiful inside, in your hearts, with the
lasting charm of a gentle and quiet spirit which
is so precious to God.

1 Peter 3:4

But all who humble themselves before the
Lord shall be given every blessing, and shall
have wonderful peace.

Psalms 37:11

A soft answer turns away wrath, but harsh
words cause quarrels.

Proverbs 15:1

Mercy

Yet the Lord still waits for you to come to him, so he can show you his love; he will conquer you to bless you, just as he said. For the Lord is faithful to his promises. Blessed are all those who wait for him to help them.

Isaiah 30:18

"Oh, that he would make you truly see yourself, for he knows everything you've done. Listen! God is doubtless punishing you far less than you deserve!"

Job 11:6

He is like a father to us, tender and sympathetic to those who reverence him.

Psalms 103:13

But the lovingkindness of the Lord is from everlasting to everlasting, to those who reverence him; his salvation is to children's children of those who are faithful to his covenant and remember to obey him!

Psalms 103:17, 18

The Lord replied, "I will make my goodness pass before you, and I will announce to you the meaning of my name Jehovah, the Lord. I show kindness and mercy to anyone I want to."

Exodus 33:19

At that time I will sow a crop of Israelites and raise them for myself! I will pity those who are "not pitied," and I will say to those who are "not my people," "Now you are my people"; and they will reply, "You are our God!"

Hosea 2:23

Foreigners will come and build your cities. Presidents and kings will send you aid. For though I destroyed you in my anger, I will have mercy on you through my grace.

Isaiah 60:10

Yet for my own sake and for the honor of my name I will hold back my anger and not wipe you out.

Isaiah 48:9

Money

Don't weary yourself trying to get rich. Why waste your time? For riches can disappear as though they had the wings of a bird!

Proverbs 23:4, 5

It is better to have little and be godly than to own an evil man's wealth.

Psalms 37:16

Listen to me, dear brothers: God has chosen poor people to be rich in faith, and the Kingdom of Heaven is theirs, for that is the gift God has promised to all those who love him.

James 2:5

The fool won't work and almost starves, but feels that it is better to be lazy and barely get by, than to work hard when, in the long run, it is all so futile.

Ecclesiastes 4:5, 6

The Lord replies, "I will arise and defend the oppressed, the poor, the needy. I will rescue them as they have longed for me to do."

Psalms 12:5

Mocking the poor is mocking the God who made them. He will punish those who rejoice at others' misfortunes.

Proverbs 17:5

Don't rob the poor and sick! For the Lord is their defender. If you injure them he will punish you.

Proverbs 22:22, 23

Tell those who are rich not to be proud and not to trust in their money, which will soon be gone, but their pride and trust should be in the living God who always richly gives us all we need for our enjoyment. Tell them to use their money to do good. They should be rich in good works and should give happily to those in need, always being ready to share with others whatever God has given them. By doing this they will be storing up real treasure for themselves in heaven — it is the only safe investment for eternity! And they will be living a fruitful Christian life down here as well.

1 Timothy 6:17–19

The man who works hard sleeps well whether he eats little or much, but the rich must worry and suffer insomnia. There is another serious problem I have seen everywhere — savings are put into risky investments that turn sour, and soon there is nothing left to pass on to one's son.

Ecclesiastes 5:12–14

"Always remember that it is the Lord your God who gives you power to become rich, and he does it to fulfill his promise to your ancestors."

Deuteronomy 8:18

"God saves the fatherless and the poor from the grasp of these oppressors. And so at last the poor have hope, and the fangs of the wicked are broken."

Job 5:15, 16

For the needs of the needy shall not be ignored forever; the hopes of the poor shall not always be crushed.

Psalms 9:18

Trust in your money and down you go! Trust in God and flourish as a tree!

Proverbs 11:28

The man who wants to do right will get a rich reward. But the man who wants to get rich quick will quickly fail.

Proverbs 28:20

Your riches won't help you on Judgment Day; only righteousness counts then.

Proverbs 11:4

"Throw away your money! Toss it out like worthless rubbish, for it will have no value in that day of wrath. It will neither satisfy nor feed you, for your love of money is the reason for your sin."

Ezekiel 7:19

Some rich people are poor, and some poor people have great wealth!

Proverbs 13:7

He who loves money shall never have enough. The foolishness of thinking that wealth brings happiness!

Ecclesiastes 5:10

He who gains by oppressing the poor or by bribing the rich shall end in poverty.

Proverbs 22:16

Trying to get rich quick is evil and leads to poverty.

Proverbs 28:22

The rich and the poor are alike before the Lord who made them all.

Proverbs 22:2

"He delivers by distress! This makes them listen to him."

Job 36:15

Better a little with reverence for God, than great treasure and trouble with it.

Proverbs 15:16

Better to be poor and honest than rich and a cheater.

Proverbs 28:6

God blesses those who are kind to the poor. He helps them out of their troubles.

Psalms 41:1

Obedience

"Look, today I have set before you life and death, depending on whether you obey or disobey. I have commanded you today to love the Lord your God and to follow his paths and to keep his laws, so that you will live and become a great nation, and so that the Lord your God will bless you and the land you are about to possess."

Deuteronomy 30:15, 16

"Only then will you be doing what is right and good in the Lord's eyes. If you obey him, all will go well for you, and you will be able to go in and possess the good land which the Lord promised your ancestors."

Deuteronomy 6:18

"Therefore, O Israel, listen closely to each command and be careful to obey it, so that all will go well with you, and so that you will have many children. If you obey these commands you will become a great nation in a glorious land 'flowing with milk and honey,' even as the God of your fathers promised you."

Deuteronomy 6:3

"Because of your obedience, the Lord your God will keep his part of the contract which, in his tender love, he made with your fathers."

Deuteronomy 7:12

"Therefore, obey the terms of this covenant so that you will prosper in everything you do."

Deuteronomy 29:9

" 'Oh, that they would always have such a heart for me, wanting to obey my commandments. Then all would go well with them in the future, and with their children throughout all generations!' "

Deuteronomy 5:29

Keep putting into practice all you learned from me and saw me doing, and the God of peace will be with you.

Philippians 4:9

"And so if anyone breaks the least commandment, and teaches others to, he shall be the least in the Kingdom of Heaven. But those who teach God's laws and obey them shall be great in the Kingdom of Heaven."

Matthew 5:19

"All who listen to my instructions and follow them are wise, like a man who builds his house on solid rock. Though the rain comes in torrents, and the floods rise and the storm winds beat against his house, it won't collapse, for it is built on rock."

Matthew 7:24, 25

"If they listen and obey him, then they will be blessed with prosperity throughout their lives."

Job 36:11

And we know that all that happens to us is working for our good if we love God and are fitting into his plans.

Romans 8:28

"When you obey me you are living in my love, just as I obey my Father and live in his love."

John 15:10

"You know these things — now do them! That is the path of blessing."

John 13:17

But if anyone keeps looking steadily into God's law for free men, he will not only remember it but he will do what it says, and God will greatly bless him in everything he does.

James 1:25

But, dearly loved friends, if our consciences are clear, we can come to the Lord with perfect assurance and trust, and get whatever we ask for because we are obeying him and doing the things that please him.

1 John 3:21, 22

He will punish sin wherever it is found. He will punish the heathen when they sin, even though they never had God's written laws, for down in their hearts they know right from wrong. God's laws are written within them; their own conscience accuses them, or sometimes excuses them. And God will punish the

Jews for sinning because they have his written laws but don't obey them. They know what is right but don't do it. After all, salvation is not given to those who know what to do, unless they do it.

Romans 2:12–15

"I say emphatically that anyone who listens to my message and believes in God who sent me has eternal life, and will never be damned for his sins, but has already passed out of death into life."

John 5:24

Then he added, "Anyone who obeys my Father in heaven is my brother, sister and mother!"

Matthew 12:50

And this world is fading away, and these evil, forbidden things will go with it, but whoever keeps doing the will of God will live forever.

1 John 2:17

"Not all who sound religious are really godly people. They may refer to me as 'Lord,' but still won't get to heaven. For the decisive question is whether they obey my Father in heaven."

Matthew 7:21

Happiness comes to those who are fair to others and are always just and good.

Psalms 106:3

It was after he had proved himself perfect in this experience that Jesus became the Giver of eternal salvation to all those who obey him.

Hebrews 5:9

"With all the earnestness I have I tell you this — no one who obeys me shall ever die!"

John 8:51

Parents' Duties

"And I have picked him out to have godly descendants and a godly household — men who are just and good — so that I can do for him all I have promised."

Genesis 18:19

I will reveal these truths to you so that you can describe these glorious deeds of Jehovah to your children, and tell them about the mighty miracles he did. For he gave his laws to Israel, and commanded our fathers to teach them to their children, so that they in turn could teach their children too. Thus his laws pass down from generation to generation.

Psalms 78:4–7

"Teach them to your children. Talk about them when you are sitting at home, when you are out walking, at bedtime, and before breakfast!"

Deuteronomy 11:19

"During those celebration days each year you must explain to your children why you are celebrating — it is a celebration of what the Lord did for you when you left Egypt."

Exodus 13:8

"But watch out! Be very careful never to forget what you have seen God doing for you. May his miracles have a deep and permanent effect upon your lives! Tell your children and your grandchildren about the glorious miracles he did. Tell them especially about the day you stood before the Lord at Mount Horeb, and he told me, 'Summon the people before me and I will instruct them, so that they will learn always to reverence me, and so that they can teach my laws to their children.' "

Deuteronomy 4:9, 10

Teach a child to choose the right path, and when he is older he will remain upon it.

Proverbs 22:6

Discipline your son and he will give you happiness and peace of mind.

Proverbs 29:17

And now a word to you parents. Don't keep on scolding and nagging your children, making them angry and resentful. Rather, bring them up with the loving discipline the Lord himself approves, with suggestions and godly advice.

Ephesians 6:4

Fathers, don't scold your children so much that they become discouraged and quit trying.

Colossians 3:21

Patience

Now as for you, dear brothers who are waiting for the Lord's return, be patient, like a farmer who waits until the autumn for his precious harvest to ripen. Yes, be patient. And take courage, for the coming of the Lord is near.

James 5:7, 8

Of course, you get no credit for being patient if you are beaten for doing wrong; but if you do right and suffer for it, and are patient beneath the blows, God is well pleased.

1 Peter 2:20

And let us not get tired of doing what is right, for after a while we will reap a harvest of blessing if we don't get discouraged and give up.

Galatians 6:9

Now we can look forward to the salvation God has promised us. There is no longer any room for doubt, and we can tell others that salvation is ours, for there is no question that he will do what he says.

Hebrews 10:23

"But those enduring to the end shall be saved."

Matthew 24:13

Then, knowing what lies ahead for you, you won't become bored with being a Christian, nor become spiritually dull and indifferent, but you will be anxious to follow the example of those who receive all that God has promised them because of their strong faith and patience.

Hebrews 6:12

You need to keep on patiently doing God's will if you want him to do for you all that he has promised.

Hebrews 10:36

Dear brothers, is your life full of difficulties and temptations? Then be happy, for when the way is rough, your patience has a chance to grow. So let it grow and don't try to squirm out of your problems. For when your patience is finally in full bloom, then you will be ready for anything, strong in character, full and complete.

James 1:2–4

We can rejoice, too, when we run into problems and trials for we know that they are good for us — they help us learn to be patient. And patience develops strength of character in us and helps us trust God more each time we use it until finally our hope and faith are strong and steady.

Romans 5:3, 4

Peace

Peace, peace to them, both near and far, for I will heal them all.

Isaiah 57:19

Let the peace of heart which comes from Christ be always present in your hearts and lives, for this is your responsibility and privilege as members of his body. And always be thankful.

Colossians 3:15

I am listening carefully to all the Lord is saying — for he speaks peace to his people, his saints, if they will only stop their sinning.

Psalms 85:8

If you do this you will experience God's peace, which is far more wonderful than the human mind can understand. His peace will keep your thoughts and your hearts quiet and at rest as you trust in Christ Jesus.

Philippians 4:7

Then justice will rule through all the land, and out of justice, peace. Quietness and confidence will reign forever more.

Isaiah 32:16, 17

And Jesus said to the woman, "Your faith has saved you; go in peace."

Luke 7:50

But the good man — what a different story! For the good man — the blameless, the upright, the man of peace — he has a wonderful future ahead of him. For him there is a happy ending.

Psalms 37:37

May the Lord of peace himself give you his peace no matter what happens. The Lord be with you all.

2 Thessalonians 3:16

"I am leaving you with a gift — peace of mind and heart! And the peace I give isn't fragile like the peace the world gives. So don't be troubled or afraid."

John 14:27

Poverty

He will take care of the helpless and poor when they cry to him; for they have no one else to defend them. He feels pity for the weak and needy, and will rescue them.

Psalms 72:12, 13

But he rescues the poor who are godly and gives them many children and much prosperity.

Psalms 107:41

For Jehovah hears the cries of his needy ones, and does not look the other way.

Psalms 69:33

Therefore I will sing out in thanks to the Lord! Praise him! For he has delivered me, poor and needy, from my oppressors.

Jeremiah 20:13

He will listen to the prayers of the destitute, for he is never too busy to heed their requests.

Psalms 102:17

Far below him are the heavens and the earth; he stoops to look, and lifts the poor from the dirt, and the hungry from the garbage dump, and sets them among princes!

Psalms 113:6–8

"I will make this city prosperous and satisfy her poor with food."

Psalms 132:15

There your people lived, for you gave them this home when thev were destitute.

Psalms 68:10

Prayer

"Ask, and you will be given what you ask for. Seek, and you will find. Knock, and the door will be opened. For everyone who asks, receives. Anyone who seeks, finds. If only you will knock, the door will open."

Matthew 7:7, 8

"You can get anything — anything you ask for in prayer — if you believe."

Matthew 21:22

O my people in Jerusalem, you shall weep no more, for he will surely be gracious to you at the sound of your cry. He will answer you.

Isaiah 30:19

And we are sure of this, that he will listen to us whenever we ask him for anything in line with his will. And if we really know he is listening when we talk to him and make our requests, then we can be sure that he will answer us.

1 John 5:14, 15

In those days when you pray, I will listen.

Jeremiah 29:12

I will answer them before they even call to me. While they are still talking to me about their needs, I will go ahead and answer their prayers!

Isaiah 65:24

"At that time you won't need to ask me for anything, for you can go directly to the Father and ask him, and he will give you what you ask for because you use my name. You haven't tried this before, [but begin now]. Ask, using my name, and you will receive, and your cup of joy will overflow."

John 16:23, 24

Admit your faults to one another and pray for each other so that you may be healed. The earnest prayer of a righteous man has great power and wonderful results.

James 5:16

"You will pray to him, and he will hear you, and you will fulfill all your promises to him."

Job 22:27

"You can ask him for anything, using my name, and I will do it, for this will bring praise to the Father because of what I, the Son, will do for you. Yes, ask anything, using my name, and I will do it!"

John 14:13, 14

"But if you stay in me and obey my commands, you may ask any request you like, and it will be granted!"

John 15:7

"But when you pray, go away by yourself, all alone, and shut the door behind you and pray to your Father secretly, and your Father, who knows your secrets, will reward you."

Matthew 6:6

I want you to trust me in your times of trouble, so I can rescue you, and you can give me glory.

Psalms 50:15

Then, when you call, the Lord will answer. "Yes, I am here," he will quickly reply. . . .

Isaiah 58:9

The Lord is far from the wicked, but he hears the prayers of the righteous.

Proverbs 15:29

"When he calls on me I will answer; I will be with him in trouble, and rescue him and honor him."

Psalms 91:15

And because you answer prayer, all mankind will come to you with their requests.

Psalms 65:2

"And if you hardhearted, sinful men know how to give good gifts to your children, won't your Father in heaven even more certainly give good gifts to those who ask him for them?"

Matthew 7:11

Yes, the Lord hears the good man when he calls to him for help, and saves him out of all his troubles.

Psalms 34:17

I will pray morning, noon, and night, plead-
ing aloud with God; and he will hear and
answer.

Psalms 55:17

He is close to all who call on him sincerely.
He fulfills the desires of those who reverence
and trust him; he hears their cries for help and
rescues them.

Psalms 145:18, 19

"I will bring the third that remain through
the fire and make them pure, as gold and silver
are refined and purified by fire. They will call
upon my name and I will hear them; I will say,
'These are my people,' and they will say, 'The
Lord is our God.' "

Zechariah 13:9

"Remember, your Father knows exactly
what you need even before you ask him."

Matthew 6:8

But, dearly loved friends, if our consciences
are clear, we can come to the Lord with perfect
assurance and trust, and get whatever we ask
for because we are obeying him and doing the
things that please him.

1 John 3:21, 22

Ask me and I will tell you some remarkable
secrets about what is going to happen here.

Jeremiah 33:3

"Listen to me! You can pray for anything, and if you believe, you have it; it's yours!"

Mark 11:24

Pride

Pride goes before destruction and haughtiness before a fall.

Proverbs 16:18

Woe to those who are wise and shrewd in their own eyes!

Isaiah 5:21

There is one thing worse than a fool, and that is a man who is conceited.

Proverbs 26:12

"Humiliate the haughty with a glance; tread down the wicked where they stand."

Job 40:12

Pride, lust, and evil actions are all sin.

Proverbs 21:4

You rebuke those cursed proud ones who refuse your commands.

Psalms 119:21

A man is a fool to trust himself! But those who use God's wisdom are safe.

Proverbs 28:26

Then he said to them, "You wear a noble, pious expression in public, but God knows your evil hearts. Your pretense brings you honor from the people, but it is an abomination in the sight of God."

Luke 16:15

If anyone respects and fears God, he will hate evil. For wisdom hates pride, arrogance, corruption and deceit of every kind.

Proverbs 8:13

Don't praise yourself; let others do it!

Proverbs 27:2

As the Scriptures say, "If anyone is going to boast, let him boast about what the Lord has done and not about himself." When someone boasts about himself and how well he has done, it doesn't count for much. But when the Lord commends him, that's different!

2 Corinthians 10:17, 18

"No wonder you can't believe! For you gladly honor each other, but you don't care about the honor that comes from the only God!"

John 5:44

He sat down and called them around him and said, "Anyone wanting to be the greatest must be the least — the servant of all!"

Mark 9:35

Prisoners

But the Lord says, "Even the captives of the most mighty and most terrible shall all be freed; for I will fight those who fight you, and I will save your children."

Isaiah 49:25

"Though you are at the ends of the earth, he will go and find you and bring you back again."

Deuteronomy 30:4

For Jehovah hears the cries of his needy ones, and does not look the other way.

Psalms 69:33

He led them from the darkness and shadow of death and snapped their chains.

Psalms 107:14

He is the God who keeps every promise, and gives justice to the poor and oppressed, and food to the hungry. He frees the prisoners.

Psalms 146:6, 7

He gives families to the lonely, and releases prisoners from jail, singing with joy! But for rebels there is famine and distress.

Psalms 68:6

God's Protection

The Lord is a strong fortress. The godly run to him and are safe.

Proverbs 18:10

"You shall laugh at war and famine; wild animals will leave you alone. Dangerous animals will be at peace with you."

Job 5:22, 23

"You will have courage because you will have hope. You will take your time, and rest in safety. You will lie down unafraid and many will look to you for help."

Job 11:18, 19

He keeps you from all evil, and preserves your life. He keeps his eye upon you as you come and go, and always guards you.

Psalms 121:7, 8

With them on guard you can sleep without fear.

Proverbs 3:24

Usually no one will hurt you for wanting to do good.

1 Peter 3:13

Concerning the tribe of Benjamin, Moses said:
"He is beloved of God
And lives in safety beside him.

God surrounds him with his loving care,
And preserves him from every harm."

Deuteronomy 33:12

He does not fear bad news, nor live in dread of what may happen. For he is settled in his mind that Jehovah will take care of him.

Psalms 112:7

For Jehovah is my refuge! I choose the God above all gods to shelter me. How then can evil overtake me or any plague come near?

Psalms 91:9, 10

But now the Lord who created you, O Israel, says, Don't be afraid, for I have ransomed you; I have called you by name; you are mine. When you go through deep waters and great trouble, I will be with you. When you go through rivers of difficulty, you will not drown! When you walk through the fire of oppression, you will not be burned up — the flames will not consume you.

Isaiah 43:1, 2

"No more will other nations conquer them nor wild animals attack. They shall live in safety and no one shall make them afraid."

Ezekiel 34:28

"But all who listen to me shall live in peace and safety, unafraid."

Proverbs 1:33

The Lord is my light and my salvation; whom shall I fear?

Psalms 27:1

I will lie down in peace and sleep, for though I am alone, O Lord, you will keep me safe.

Psalms 4:8

Repentance

"At last the time has come!" he announced. "God's Kingdom is near! Turn from your sins and act on this glorious news!"

Mark 1:15

So the disciples went out, telling everyone they met to turn from sin.

Mark 6:12

The Lord is close to those whose hearts are breaking; he rescues those who are humbly sorry for their sins.

Psalms 34:18

He heals the brokenhearted, binding up their wounds.

Psalms 147:3

"Before you turn to God and stretch out your hands to him, get rid of your sins and leave all iniquity behind you. Only then, without the spots of sin to defile you, can you walk steadily forward to God without fear."

Job 11:13–15

"But if a wicked person turns away from all his sins and begins to obey my laws and do what is just and right, he shall surely live and not die. All his past sins will be forgotten, and he shall live because of his goodness."

Ezekiel 18:21, 22

". . . For I have come to urge sinners, not the self-righteous, back to God."

Matthew 9:13

Righteousness

For Jehovah God is our Light and our Protector. He gives us grace and glory. No good thing will he withhold from those who walk along his paths.

Psalms 84:11

Even strong young lions sometimes go hungry, but those of us who reverence the Lord will never lack any good thing.

Psalms 34:10

The wicked man's fears will all come true, and so will the good man's hopes.

Proverbs 10:24

Curses chase sinners, while blessings chase the righteous!

Proverbs 13:21

Wickedness never brings real success; only the godly have that.

Proverbs 12:2

". . . But your heavenly Father already knows perfectly well that you need them, and he will give them to you if you give him first place in your life and live as he wants you to."

Matthew 6:32, 33

Trust in your money and down you go! Trust in God and flourish as a tree!

Proverbs 11:28

Then at last everyone will know that good is rewarded, and that there is a God who judges justly here on earth.

Psalms 58:11

For you bless the godly man, O Lord; you protect him with your shield of love.

Psalms 5:12

For salvation comes from God. What joys he gives to all his people.

Psalms 3:8

He has given you the whole world to use, and life and even death are your servants. He has given you all of the present and all of the future. All are yours, and you belong to Christ, and Christ is God's.

1 Corinthians 3:22, 23

Since he did not spare even his own Son for us but gave him up for us all, won't he also surely give us everything else?

Romans 8:32

But all is well for the godly man. Tell him, "What a reward you are going to get!"

Isaiah 3:10

Your goodness and unfailing kindness shall be with me all of my life, and afterwards I will live with you forever in your home.

Psalms 23:6

Salvation

Jesus replied, "With all the earnestness I possess I tell you this: Unless you are born again, you can never get into the Kingdom of God."

"Born again!" exclaimed Nicodemus. "What do you mean? How can an old man go back into his mother's womb and be born again?"

Jesus replied, "What I am telling you so earnestly is this: Unless one is born of water and the Spirit, he cannot enter the Kingdom of God. Men can only reproduce human life, but the Holy Spirit gives new life from heaven; so don't be surprised at my statement that you must be born again!"

John 3:3-7

When someone becomes a Christian he becomes a brand new person inside. He is not the same any more. A new life has begun!

2 Corinthians 5:17

For God took the sinless Christ and poured into him our sins. Then, in exchange, he poured God's goodness into us!

2 Corinthians 5:21

Once you were under God's curse, doomed forever for your sins.

Ephesians 2:1

This is good and pleases God our Savior, for he longs for all to be saved and to understand this truth: That God is on one side and all the people on the other side, and Christ Jesus, himself man, is between them to bring them together, by giving his life for all mankind.

1 Timothy 2:3–6

My little children, I am telling you this so that you will stay away from sin. But if you sin, there is someone to plead for you before the Father. His name is Jesus Christ, the one who is all that is good and who pleases God completely. He is the one who took God's wrath against our sins upon himself, and brought us into fellowship with God; and he is the forgiveness for our sins, and not only ours but all the world's.

1 John 2:1, 2

You were dead in sins, and your sinful desires were not yet cut away. Then he gave you a share in the very life of Christ, for he forgave all your sins.

Colossians 2:13

This is the truth and everyone should accept it. We work hard and suffer much in order that people will believe it, for our hope is in the living God who died for all, and particularly for those who have accepted his salvation.

1 Timothy 4:9, 10

. . . What a contrast between Adam and Christ who was yet to come! And what a difference between man's sin and God's forgiveness! For this one man, Adam, brought death to many through his sin. But this one man, Jesus Christ, brought forgiveness to many through God's mercy.

Romans 5:14, 15

But when the time came for the kindness and love of God our Savior to appear, then he saved us — not because we were good enough to be saved, but because of his kindness and pity — by washing away our sins and giving us the new joy of the indwelling Holy Spirit whom he poured out upon us with wonderful fullness — and all because of what Jesus Christ our Savior did.

Titus 3:4–6

But to all who received him, he gave the right to become children of God. All they needed to do was to trust him to save them. All those who believe this are reborn! — not a physical rebirth resulting from human passion or plan — but from the will of God.

John 1:12, 13

Seeking God

"The Lord will stay with you as long as you stay with him! Whenever you look for him, you will find him. But if you forsake him, he will forsake you."

2 Chronicles 15:2

Plant the good seeds of righteousness and you will reap a crop of my love; plow the hard ground of your hearts, for now is the time to seek the Lord, that he may come and shower salvation upon you.

Hosea 10:12

You can never please God without faith, without depending on him. Anyone who wants to come to God must believe that there is a God and that he rewards those who sincerely look for him.

Hebrews 11:6

"His purpose in all of this is that they should seek after God, and perhaps feel their way toward him and find him — though he is not far from any one of us."

Acts 17:27

The Lord is wonderfully good to those who wait for him, to those who seek for him.

Lamentations 3:25

The Lord says to the people of Israel, "Seek me — and live."

Amos 5:4

"But you will also begin to search again for Jehovah your God, and you shall find him when you search for him with all your hearts and souls."

Deuteronomy 4:29

. . . After all, we had told the king that our God would protect all those who worshiped him, and that disaster could come only to those who had forsaken him!

Ezra 8:22

"Solomon, my son, get to know the God of your fathers. Worship and serve him with a clean heart and a willing mind, for the Lord sees every heart and understands and knows every thought. If you seek him, you will find him; but if you forsake him, he will permanently throw you aside."

1 Chronicles 28:9

"If your children sinned against him, and he punished them, and you begged Almighty God for them — if you were pure and good, he would hear your prayer, and answer you, and bless you with a happy home."

Job 8:4–6

All those who know your mercy, Lord, will count on you for help. For you have never yet forsaken those who trust in you.

Psalms 9:10

You will find me when you seek me, if you look for me in earnest.

Jeremiah 29:13

Self-Denial

Then Jesus said to the disciples, "If anyone wants to be a follower of mine, let him deny himself and take up his cross and follow me. For anyone who keeps his life for himself shall lose it; and anyone who loses his life for me shall find it again. What profit is there if you gain the whole world — and lose eternal life? What can be compared with the value of eternal life?"

Matthew 16:24–26

So dear brothers, you have no obligations whatever to your old sinful nature to do what it begs you to do. For if you keep on following it you are lost and will perish, but if through the power of the Holy Spirit you crush it and its evil deeds, you shall live.

Romans 8:12, 13

Those who belong to Christ have nailed their natural evil desires to his cross and crucified them there.

Galatians 5:24

For the free gift of eternal salvation is now being offered to everyone; and along with this gift comes the realization that God wants us to turn from godless living and sinful pleasures and to live good, God-fearing lives day after day.

Titus 2:11, 12

"But I say: Don't resist violence! If you are slapped on one cheek, turn the other too. If you are ordered to court, and your shirt is taken from you, give your coat too. If the military demand that you carry their gear for a mile, carry it two."

Matthew 5:39–41

"Yes," Jesus replied, "and everyone who has done as you have, leaving home, wife, brothers, parents, or children for the sake of the Kingdom of God, will be repaid many times over now, as well as receiving eternal life in the world to come."

Luke 18:29, 30

Self-Righteousness

"You have said it in my hearing, yes, you've said it again and again — 'I am pure, I am innocent; I have not sinned.' "

Job 33:8, 9

"Do you think it is right for you to claim, 'I haven't sinned, but I'm no better off before God than if I had'?"

Job 35:2

Woe to those who are wise and shrewd in their own eyes!

Isaiah 5:21

"But it is false to say he doesn't hear those cries; and it is even more false to say that he doesn't see what is going on. He does bring about justice at last, if you will only wait. But do you cry out against him because he does not instantly respond in anger? Job, you have spoken like a fool."

Job 35:13–16

There is one thing worse than a fool, and that is a man who is conceited.

Proverbs 26:12

If anyone thinks he is too great to stoop to this, he is fooling himself. He is really a nobody.

Galatians 6:3

As the Scriptures say, "If anyone is going to boast, let him boast about what the Lord has done and not about himself." When someone boasts about himself and how well he has done, it doesn't count for much. But when the Lord commends him, that's different!

2 Corinthians 10:17, 18

"If you were blind, you wouldn't be guilty," Jesus replied. "But your guilt remains because you claim to know what you are doing."

John 9:41

We are all infected and impure with sin. When we put on our prized robes of righteousness we find they are but filthy rags. Like autumn leaves we fade, wither and fall. And our sins, like the wind, sweep us away.

Isaiah 64:6

Greed causes fighting; trusting God leads to prosperity. A man is a fool to trust himself! But those who use God's wisdom are safe.

Proverbs 28:25, 26

Then he said to them, "You wear a noble, pious expression in public, but God knows your evil hearts. Your pretense brings you honor from the people, but it is an abomination in the sight of God."

Luke 16:15

Don't praise yourself; let others do it!

Proverbs 27:2

Sexual Sins

. . . But sexual sin is never right: our bodies were not made for that, but for the Lord, and the Lord wants to fill our bodies with himself.

1 Corinthians 6:13

That is why I say to run from sex sin. No other sin affects the body as this one does. When you sin this sin it is against your own body. Haven't you yet learned that your body is the home of the Holy Spirit God gave you, and that he lives within you? Your own body does not belong to you. For God has bought you with a great price. So use every part of your body to give glory back to God, because he owns it.

1 Corinthians 6:18–20

Now about those questions you asked in your last letter: my answer is that if you do not marry, it is good.

1 Corinthians 7:1

So I say to those who aren't married, and to widows — better to stay unmarried if you can, just as I am. But if you can't control yourselves, go ahead and marry. It is better to marry than to burn with lust.

1 Corinthians 7:8, 9

But if a man has the willpower not to marry and decides that he doesn't need to and won't, he has made a wise decision.

1 Corinthians 7:37

But remember this — the wrong desires that come into your life aren't anything new and different. Many others have faced exactly the same problems before you. And no temptation is irresistible. You can trust God to keep the temptation from becoming so strong that you can't stand up against it, for he has promised this and will do what he says. He will show you how to escape temptation's power so that you can bear up patiently against it.

1 Corinthians 10:13

For they are spiritually undefiled, pure as virgins, following the Lamb wherever he goes. They have been purchased from among the men on the earth as a consecrated offering to God and the Lamb.

Revelation 14:4

For God wants you to be holy and pure, and to keep clear of all sexual sin.

1 Thessalonians 4:3

Honor your marriage and its vows, and be pure; for God will surely punish all those who are immoral or commit adultery.

Hebrews 13:4

Don't you realize that your bodies are actually parts and members of Christ? So should I take part of Christ and join him to a prostitute? Never!

1 Corinthians 6:15

If you can find a truly good wife, she is worth more than precious gems!

Proverbs 31:10

So also the Lord can rescue you and me from the temptations that surround us, and continue to punish the ungodly until the day of final judgment comes.

2 Peter 2:9

Happy is the man who doesn't give in and do wrong when he is tempted, for afterwards he will get as his reward the crown of life that God has promised those who love him.

James 1:12

For since he himself has now been through suffering and temptation, he knows what it is like when we suffer and are tempted, and he is wonderfully able to help us.

Hebrews 2:18

This High Priest of ours understands our weaknesses, since he had the same temptations we do, though he never once gave way to them and sinned. So let us come boldly to the very throne of God and stay there to receive his mercy and to find grace to help us in our times of need.

Hebrews 4:15, 16

Shame

For the Scriptures tell us that no one who believes in Christ will ever be disappointed.

Romans 10:11

Then I will not be disgraced, for I will have a clean record.

Psalms 119:6

Then, when that happens, we are able to hold our heads high no matter what happens and know that all is well, for we know how dearly God loves us, and we feel this warm love everywhere within us because God has given us the Holy Spirit to fill our hearts with his love.

Romans 5:5

That is why I am suffering here in jail and I am certainly not ashamed of it, for I know the one in whom I trust, and I am sure that he is able to safely guard all that I have given him until the day of his return.

2 Timothy 1:12

God warned them of this in the Scriptures when he said, ''I have put a Rock in the path of the Jews, and many will stumble over him (Jesus). Those who believe in him will never be disappointed.''

Romans 9:33

Work hard so God can say to you, "Well done." Be a good workman, one who does not need to be ashamed when God examines your work. Know what his Word says and means.

2 Timothy 2:15

Help me to love your every wish; then I will never have to be ashamed of myself.

Psalms 119:80

But it is no shame to suffer for being a Christian. Praise God for the privilege of being in Christ's family and being called by his wonderful name!

1 Peter 4:16

Sickness

Is anyone sick? He should call for the elders of the church and they should pray over him and pour a little oil upon him, calling on the Lord to heal him. And their prayer, if offered in faith, will heal him, for the Lord will make him well; and if his sickness was caused by some sin, the Lord will forgive him. Admit your faults to one another and pray for each other so that you may be healed. The earnest prayer of a righteous man has great power and wonderful results.

James 5:14–16

They went right into the house where he was staying, and Jesus asked them, "Do you believe I can make you see?"

"Yes, Lord," they told him, "we do."

Then he touched their eyes and said, "Because of your faith it will happen."

And suddenly they could see!

Matthew 9:28–30

Lord, you alone can heal me, you alone can save, and my praises are for you alone.

Jeremiah 17:14

"I, the Messiah, have the authority on earth to forgive sins. But talk is cheap — anybody could say that. So I'll prove it to you by healing this man." Then, turning to the paralyzed man, he commanded, "Pick up your stretcher and go on home, for you are healed." And the boy jumped up and left!

Matthew 9:5–7

I will give you back your health again and heal your wounds.

Jeremiah 30:17

"You shall serve the Lord your God only; then I will bless you with food and with water, and I will take away sickness from among you."

Exodus 23:25

He personally carried the load of our sins in his own body when he died on the cross, so that we can be finished with sin and live a good life from now on. For his wounds have healed ours!

1 Peter 2:24

But he was wounded and bruised for our sins. He was chastised that we might have peace; he was lashed — and we were healed!

Isaiah 53:5

Freedom From Sin

"Then it will be as though I had sprinkled clean water on you, for you will be clean — your filthiness will be washed away, your idol worship gone. And I will give you a new heart — I will give you new and right desires — and put a new spirit within you. I will take out your stony hearts of sin and give you new hearts of love."

Ezekiel 36:25, 26

"And all the prophets have written about him, saying that everyone who believes in him will have their sins forgiven through his name."

Acts 10:43

Your old evil desires were nailed to the cross with him; that part of you that loves to sin was crushed and fatally wounded, so that your sin-loving body is no longer under sin's control, no longer needs to be a slave to sin; for when you are deadened to sin you are freed from all its allure and its power over you.

Romans 6:6, 7

When someone becomes a Christian he becomes a brand new person inside. He is not the same any more. A new life has begun!

2 Corinthians 5:17

Well then, shall we keep on sinning so that God can keep on showing us more and more kindness and forgiveness? Of course not! Should we keep on sinning when we don't have to? For sin's power over us was broken when we became Christians and were baptized to become a part of Jesus Christ; through his death the power of your sinful nature was shattered.

Romans 6:1–3

So look upon your old sin nature as dead and unresponsive to sin, and instead be alive to God, alert to him, through Jesus Christ our Lord.

Romans 6:11

Sin need never again be your master, for now you are no longer tied to the law where sin enslaves you, but you are free under God's favor and mercy.

Romans 6:14

Redemption From Sin

"And she will have a Son, and you shall name him Jesus (meaning 'Savior'), for he will save his people from their sins."

Matthew 1:21

"Brothers! Listen! In this man Jesus, there is forgiveness for your sins!"

Acts 13:38

And you know that he became a man so that he could take away our sins, and that there is no sin in him, no missing of God's will at any time in any way.

1 John 3:5

My little children, I am telling you this so that you will stay away from sin. But if you sin, there is someone to plead for you before the Father. His name is Jesus Christ, the one who is all that is good and who pleases God completely. He is the one who took God's wrath against our sins upon himself, and brought us into fellowship with God; and he is the forgiveness for our sins, and not only ours but all the world's.

1 John 2:1, 2

He personally carried the load of our sins in his own body when he died on the cross, so that we can be finished with sin and live a

good life from now on. For his wounds have
healed ours!

1 Peter 2:24

How true it is, and how I long that everyone
should know it, that Christ Jesus came into the
world to save sinners — and I was the greatest
of them all.

1 Timothy 1:15

But he was wounded and bruised for our
sins. He was chastised that we might have
peace; he was lashed — and we were healed!
We are the ones who strayed away like sheep!
We, who left God's paths to follow our own.
Yet God laid on him the guilt and sins of every
one of us!

Isaiah 53:5, 6

The next day John saw Jesus coming toward
him and said, "Look! There is the Lamb of
God who takes away the world's sin!"

John 1:29

So overflowing is his kindness towards us
that he took away all our sins through the
blood of his Son, by whom we are saved.

Ephesians 1:7

He died for our sins just as God our Father
planned, and rescued us from this evil world in
which we live.

Galatians 1:4

So also Christ died only once as an offering for the sins of many people; and he will come again, but not to deal again with our sins. This time he will come bringing salvation to all those who are eagerly and patiently waiting for him.

Hebrews 9:28

For by that one offering he made forever perfect in the sight of God all those whom he is making holy.

Hebrews 10:14

"For this is my blood, sealing the New Covenant. It is poured out to forgive the sins of multitudes."

Matthew 26:28

Slander and Reproach

"When you are reviled and persecuted and lied about because you are my followers — wonderful! Be happy about it! Be very glad! for a tremendous reward awaits you up in heaven. And remember, the ancient prophets were persecuted too."

Matthew 5:11, 12

Be happy if you are cursed and insulted for being a Christian, for when that happens the Spirit of God will come upon you with great glory.

1 Peter 4:14

He will send down help from heaven to save me, because of his love and his faithfulness. He will rescue me from these liars who are so intent upon destroying me.

Psalms 57:3

Listen to me, you who know the right from wrong and cherish my laws in your hearts: don't be afraid of people's scorn or their slanderous talk.

Isaiah 51:7

Hide your loved ones in the shelter of your presence, safe beneath your hand, safe from all conspiring men.

Psalms 31:20

"You will be safe from slander; no need to fear the future."

Job 5:21

Your innocence will be clear to everyone. He will vindicate you with the blazing light of justice shining down as from the noonday sun.

Psalms 37:6

Success

There is treasure in being good, but trouble dogs the wicked.

Proverbs 15:6

True humility and respect for the Lord lead a man to riches, honor and long life.

Proverbs 22:4

"The Lord your God will prosper everything you do and give you many children and much cattle and wonderful crops; for the Lord will again rejoice over you as he did over your fathers."

Deuteronomy 30:9

Then God will bless you with rain at planting time and with wonderful harvests and with ample pastures for your cows.

Isaiah 30:23

"The Lord will give you an abundance of good things in the land, just as he promised: many children, many cattle, and abundant crops. He will open to you his wonderful treasury of rain in the heavens, to give you fine crops every season. He will bless everything you do; and you shall lend to many nations, but shall not borrow from them. If you will only listen and obey the commandments of the Lord your God that I am giving you today, he will make you the head and not the tail, and you shall always have the upper hand.''

Deuteronomy 28:11–13

And, of course, it is very good if a man has received wealth from the Lord, and the good health to enjoy it. To enjoy your work and to accept your lot in life — that is indeed a gift from God.

Ecclesiastes 5:19

And second, that he should eat and drink and enjoy the fruits of his labors, for these are gifts from God.

Ecclesiastes 3:13

''Whatever you wish will happen! And the light of heaven will shine upon the road ahead of you.''

Job 22:28

''Unending riches, honor, justice and righteousness are mine to distribute. My gifts are better than the purest gold or sterling silver!''

Proverbs 8:18, 19

He himself shall be wealthy, and his good deeds will never be forgotten.

Psalms 112:3

''He will give you lush pastureland for your cattle to graze in, and you yourselves shall have plenty to eat and be fully content.''

Deuteronomy 11:15

"If you give up your lust for money, and throw your gold away, then the Almighty himself shall be your treasure; he will be your precious silver!"

Job 22:24, 25

Blessings on all who reverence and trust the Lord — on all who obey him! Their reward shall be prosperity and happiness.

Psalms 128:1, 2

In those days, when a man builds a house, he will keep on living in it — it will not be destroyed by invading armies as in the past. My people will plant vineyards and eat the fruit themselves — their enemies will not confiscate it. For my people will live as long as trees and will long enjoy their hard-won gains. Their harvests will not be eaten by their enemies; their children will not be born to be cannon fodder. For they are the children of those the Lord has blessed; and their children, too, shall be blessed.

Isaiah 65:21–23

They are like trees along a river bank bearing luscious fruit each season without fail. Their leaves shall never wither, and all they do shall prosper.

Psalms 1:3

"These are the blessings that will come upon you:
   Blessings in the city,
   Blessings in the field;
   Many children,
   Ample crops,
   Large flocks and herds;
   Blessings of fruit and bread;
   Blessings when you come in,
   Blessings when you go out."

Deuteronomy 28:2–6

Trust

God is our refuge and strength, a tested help in times of trouble. And so we need not fear even if the world blows up, and the mountains crumble into the sea.

Psalms 46:1, 2

For Jehovah God is our Light and our Protector. He gives us grace and glory. No good thing will he withhold from those who walk along his paths. O Lord of the armies of heaven, blessed are those who trust in you.

Psalms 84:11, 12

Trust in the Lord instead. Be kind and good to others; then you will live safely here in the land and prosper, feeding in safety. Be delighted with the Lord. Then he will give you all your heart's desires. Commit everything you do to the Lord. Trust him to help you do it and he will.

Psalms 37:3–5

Trust the Lord completely; don't ever trust yourself. In everything you do, put God first, and he will direct you and crown your efforts with success.

Proverbs 3:5, 6

"So don't be afraid, little flock. For it gives your Father great happiness to give you the Kingdom."

Luke 12:32

"So don't worry at all about having enough food and clothing. Why be like the heathen? For they take pride in all these things and are deeply concerned about them."

Matthew 6:31, 32

Let him have all your worries and cares, for he is always thinking about you and watching everything that concerns you.

1 Peter 5:7

Many blessings are given to those who trust the Lord, and have no confidence in those who are proud, or who trust in idols.

Psalms 40:4

Those who trust in the Lord are steady as Mount Zion, unmoved by any circumstance.

Psalms 125:1

Wisdom

If you want to know what God wants you to do, ask him, and he will gladly tell you, for he is always ready to give a bountiful supply of wisdom to all who ask him; he will not resent it.

James 1:5

"Come," everyone will say, "let us go up the mountain of the Lord, to the Temple of the God of Israel; there he will teach us his laws, and we will obey them."

Isaiah 2:3

I will instruct you (says the Lord) and guide you along the best pathway for your life; I will advise you and watch your progress.

Psalms 32:8

For God gives those who please him wisdom, knowledge, and joy.

Ecclesiastes 2:26

I will bless the Lord who counsels me; he gives me wisdom in the night. He tells me what to do.

Psalms 16:7

Yes, if you want better insight and discernment, and are searching for them as you would for lost money or hidden treasure, then wisdom will be given you, and knowledge of

God himself; you will soon learn the importance of reverence for the Lord and of trusting him. For the Lord grants wisdom! His every word is a treasure of knowledge and understanding. He grants good sense to the godly — his saints. He is their shield, protecting them and guarding their pathway.

Proverbs 2:3–8

And we know that Christ, God's Son, has come to help us understand and find the true God. And now we are in God because we are in Jesus Christ his Son, who is the only true God; and he is eternal Life.

1 John 5:20

For God, who said, "Let there be light in the darkness," has made us understand that it is the brightness of his glory that is seen in the face of Jesus Christ.

2 Corinthians 4:6

Evil men don't understand the importance of justice, but those who follow the Lord are much concerned about it.

Proverbs 28:5

You deserve honesty from the heart; yes, utter sincerity and truthfulness. Oh, give me this wisdom.

Psalms 51:6

Word of God

For I am not ashamed of this Good News about Christ. It is God's powerful method of bringing all who believe it to heaven. This message was preached first to the Jews alone, but now everyone is invited to come to God in this same way.

Romans 1:16

If you read this prophecy aloud to the church, you will receive a special blessing from the Lord. Those who listen to it being read and do what it says will also be blessed. For the time is near when these things will all come true.

Revelation 1:3

So we have seen and proved that what the prophets said came true. You will do well to pay close attention to everything they have written, for, like lights shining into dark corners, their words help us to understand many things that otherwise would be dark and difficult. But when you consider the wonderful truth of the prophets' words, then the light will dawn in your souls and Christ the Morning Star will shine in your hearts.

2 Peter 1:19

For whatever God says to us is full of living power: it is sharper than the sharpest dagger,

cutting swift and deep into our innermost
thoughts and desires with all their parts, expos-
ing us for what we really are.

Hebrews 4:12

As your plan unfolds, even the simple can
understand it.

Psalms 119:130

For their advice is a beam of light directed
into the dark corners of your mind to warn you
of danger and to give you a good life.

Proverbs 6:23

Your words are a flashlight to light the path
ahead of me, and keep me from stumbling.

Psalms 119:105

"You search the Scriptures, for you believe
they give you eternal life. And the Scriptures
point to me!"

John 5:39

You know how, when you were a small
child, you were taught the holy Scriptures; and
it is these that make you wise to accept God's
salvation by trusting in Christ Jesus. The
whole Bible was given to us by inspiration from
God and is useful to teach us what is true and
to make us realize what is wrong in our lives; it
straightens us out and helps us do what is right.

2 Timothy 3:15, 16

Yet faith comes from listening to this Good News — the Good News about Christ.

Romans 10:17

Now that you realize how kind the Lord has been to you, put away all evil, deception, envy, and fraud. Long to grow up into the fullness of your salvation; cry for this as a baby cries for his milk.

1 Peter 2:2, 3

So get rid of all that is wrong in your life, both inside and outside, and humbly be glad for the wonderful message we have received, for it is able to save our souls as it takes hold of our hearts. And remember, it is a message to obey, not just to listen to. So don't fool yourselves. For if a person just listens and doesn't obey, he is like a man looking at his face in a mirror; as soon as he walks away, he can't see himself anymore or remember what he looks like. But if anyone keeps looking steadily into God's law for free men, he will not only remember it but he will do what it says, and God will greatly bless him in everything he does.

James 1:21–25

"So keep these commandments carefully in mind. Tie them to your hand to remind you to obey them, and tie them to your forehead between your eyes!"

Deuteronomy 11:18

"Constantly remind the people about these laws, and you yourself must think about them every day and every night so that you will be sure to obey all of them. For only then will you succeed."

Joshua 1:8

For you have a new life. It was not passed on to you from your parents, for the life they gave you will fade away. This new one will last forever, for it comes from Christ, God's ever-living Message to men.

1 Peter 1:23

"And now I entrust you to God and his care and to his wonderful words which are able to build your faith and give you all the inheritance of those who are set apart for himself."

Acts 20:32

NOTES

THE CHRISTIAN LIBRARY

Classics of the Christian faith in deluxe, hardcover, gold stamped, gift editions. These beautifully crafted volumes are in matching burgundy leatherette bindings so you can purchase a complete set or pick and choose. All books are complete and unabridged and are printed in good readable print.   Only $7.99 each!

ABIDE IN CHRIST, Andrew Murray
BEN-HUR: A TALE OF THE CHRIST, Lew Wallace
THE CHRISTIAN'S SECRET OF A HAPPY LIFE,
Hannah Whitall Smith
CONFESSIONS OF ST. AUGUSTINE
DAILY LIGHT, Samuel Bagster
EACH NEW DAY, Corrie ten Boom
FOXE'S CHRISTIAN MARTYRS OF THE WORLD,
John Foxe
GOD AT EVENTIDE, A.J. Russell
GOD CALLING, A.J. Russell
THE GOD OF ALL COMFORT, Hannah Whitall Smith
GOD'S SMUGGLER, Brother Andrew
THE HIDING PLACE, Corrie ten Boom
HINDS' FEET ON HIGH PLACES, Hannah Hurnard
THE IMITATION OF CHRIST, Thomas à Kempis
IN HIS STEPS, Charles M. Sheldon
MERE CHRISTIANITY, C.S. Lewis
MY UTMOST FOR HIS HIGHEST, Oswald Chambers
THE PILGRIM'S PROGRESS, John Bunyan
POWER THROUGH PRAYER/PURPOSE IN PRAYER,
E.M. Bounds
QUIET TALKS ON PRAYER, S.D. Gordon
THE SCREWTAPE LETTERS, C.S. Lewis
WHO'S WHO IN THE BIBLE, Frank S. Mead

*Available at your friendly Christian booksore,
a wonderful place to visit!*

or order from:

Barbour and Company, Inc.
P.O. Box 719
Uhrichsville, Ohio 44683

ISBN 1-55748-598-4